Violence, Silence, and Rhetorical Cultures of Champion-Building in Sports

This book takes a close look at systems and rhetorics of silencing in sports training. Using the case study of the Larry Nassar abuse scandal at Michigan State University and within USA Gymnastics, the book explores multifaceted problems of speaking, silencing, and listening in youth and college athletic organizations, investigating the cultures of abuse and discursive practices that silence victims while protecting abusers.

The author foregrounds the victims' voices through an analysis of victim impact statements and victim interviews, while examining other textual artifacts to understand the institutional behaviors and actions both before and after the case caught public attention. Exploring the issue far beyond the single organization, the author discusses the norms, values, ideologies, and expected behaviors of youth and college sports programs as institutions to help describe "rhetorical cultures of champion-building."

This innovative study offers new perspectives that will interest students and scholars of sport communication, rhetoric, organizational communication, criminology, and feminist theory.

Kathleen Sandell Hardesty teaches English and technical communication at Florida Polytechnic University. She has also worked as a technical writer/editor and communications consultant for the engineering industry.

Routledge Studies in Rhetoric and Communication

Violence, Silence, and Rhetorical Cultures of Champion-Building in Sports

Kathleen Sandell Hardesty

Routledge
Taylor & Francis Group

NEW YORK AND LONDON

First published 2023
by Routledge
605 Third Avenue, New York, NY 10158

and by Routledge
4 Park Square, Milton Park, Abingdon, Oxon, OX14 4RN

Routledge is an imprint of the Taylor & Francis Group, an informa business

ISBN: 978-1-032-38273-9 (hbk)
ISBN: 978-1-032-39466-4 (pbk)
ISBN: 978-1-003-34984-6 (ebk)

DOI: 10.4324/9781003349846

Typeset in Times New Roman
by codeMantra

To John and Cora. You are my greatest joy.
And for the Army of Survivors, who are still fighting for justice and whose voices matter.

Contents

Figures

Tables

Acknowledgments

I am deeply grateful to the kind and brilliant scholars who empowered this research in its origins as my dissertation for Texas Tech University's Technical Communication and Rhetoric program: Dr. Rebecca Rickly, Dr. Kendall Gerdes, and Dr. Eileen Farchmin. Thank you for your guidance, encouragement, and support throughout this project.

I am thankful for the many friends, family, and colleagues who have encouraged me on this journey. In particular, I am grateful for the TCR Fam—Kristine Acosta, Kimberly Fain, Andrew Hollinger, Delphine Broccard Jimenez, Jessica Weber Metzenroth, and Manny Piña—for the laughs, support, insight, and friendship you have brought to our doctoral program and far beyond. Special thanks to Dr. Fain for her wisdom and mentorship—and the extra nudges I needed—in the book proposal process.

I owe endless thanks to my husband, Craig, for being by my side and for giving me the space and strength to see this effort through to the end. I know love for knowing you. Life began again the day you took my hand.

With appreciation to my parents, Bruce and Allene, for your love and support. Thank you for believing in me, always.

To the Army of Survivors who are still fighting for justice and for change: fight on. This is a book about your voices, and your voices are making a difference. To you, we owe our never-ending thanks.

1 Introduction

Violence, silence, and athletics

At just 7 years old, my daughter began training for the USA Gymnastics Talent Opportunity Program (TOPs). All over the United States, TOPs gymnasts practice a series of strenuous physical abilities—such as press handstands, handstand holds, and arms-only rope climbs—in preparation for state and regional testing to earn a spot on the TOPs national teams. During one of my daughter's first sessions, I was seated in the gym's parent viewing area, not particularly paying attention to the practice, when my daughter came up and told me that her coach wanted me to leave. Startled, I did something I regret to this day. I left.

Later that evening, still angry and concerned over what had transpired at the practice, I agonized over whether to contact her coach, since I truly did not know why I was asked to leave. Was she worried that I would cause a distraction? Was she anticipating that I would be anxious about the more aggressive training for TOPs? Was it something worse? In social situations, my daughter, who is adopted, occasionally glances at me or runs up to me briefly to reassure herself that I am there. At the time, it was not something that most children her age did, but it was something she uniquely needed. Since the coach did not know the details of my daughter's early history, I generously assumed that she could not have known how inappropriate it was to send *my daughter* to tell *me* to go away. In the end, I made a second decision that I regret. Worried that questioning the coach would lead to negative consequences against my daughter and/or potentially end her TOPs training, I chose not to challenge the action. Against my better judgment as a parent, acquiescing to the unsupervised training of my underage child with an adult in techniques I was not familiar with, I did not speak up.

A few months later, I watched HBO's documentary on USA Gymnastics and Larry Nassar, *At the Heart of Gold.* The documentary offers a different perspective into the highly publicized

DOI: 10.4324/9781003349846-1

Larry Nassar abuse scandal (discussed at length later). The director centers the story on various voices connected to USA Gymnastics and Nassar through snippets of interviews. Olympic gymnast Dominique Moceanu summed up her training culture during one of the interviews in five memorable words: "you better not speak up." Recalling her training with USA Gymnastics coaches Béla and Márta Károlyi at the National Team Training Center on their secluded ranch in Texas, Moceanu remarked: "Doesn't matter if you're injured. 'You better not speak up' was the whole mentality in the environment. You'd better not or else we're going to take your Olympic dream away" (HBO, 2019, 13:40). During this training, Moceanu, just 14 years old and a minor, was not permitted access to her parents or anyone outside the training facility. Together, Moceanu's voice and others paint a pretty chilling picture of the cultures and institutions that enabled, cultivated, and protected a sexual predator. Watching the details of the USA Gymnastics scandal unfold and listening to the testimony of gymnasts and their parents left me with many difficult feelings, but one particularly unsettling truth was that I could see exactly how this could happen, even from my limited observations. I have personally observed a reluctance among parents (including myself) to voice perfectly legitimate concerns about their children's training or safety—or even to ask questions—for fear of negative consequences. And unfortunately, I would not consider this experience at all unusual for highly competitive teams. Why are we all so afraid to speak up?

In my experience, and based on numerous texts found on gym webpages, blogs, training advice columns, and other media, many elite and non-elite gymnastics training programs have traditionally encouraged a separation of parent and gymnast. "Gymnastics is a 'special' sport that really is a hand's [sic] off for parents," says Emeth Gymnastics of their TOPs Program ("TOPS – Emeth Gymnastics," n.d.). Later, during my daughter's competition season, her coach again approached me, as she had noticed my daughter's tendency to glance at me in the stands during a competition. Seeing the glances as evidence of a lack of concentration (or perhaps of me trying to "coach her from the stands"), her coach suggested that I move around and essentially "hide" from my daughter during competition. In another blog shared on my daughter's gym Facebook page, the blogger tells her story of her challenges as the mother of a gymnast and the moment she decided "'WE' were no longer going to do gymnastics" (Brown, 2017). During a competition, she looked down at her young daughter and the mats she needed to stand on to be tall enough to even mount the beam and "looked at those judges waiting to judge my tiny little daughter and my heart said, 'F*&$ this!'" Did she follow her heart and decide to quit the sport to protect her little daughter? No. She decided to remove the "me" part of "we," to remove herself from her daughter's gymnastics training and competition. Describing (triumphantly) her daughter's subsequent gymnastics experience, she writes:

> She pushed through severs, and broken fingers, broken toes, and beam bites. She worked out sick. She worked out while others played. She competed scared. She competed injured. She competed strong. She woke up early and she stayed up late.

Later, she describes her role as a gymnast's parent as consisting of activities like getting her daughter to the gym on time; making sure she is fed, hydrated, rested, and ready to train; and cheering at meets.

Admittedly, it is difficult to find the perfect balance in parenting an athlete in a sport, and few sports are as physically challenging as gymnastics. Juliet Macur, a journalist for *The New York Times,* says:

> I don't think there's a sport that's harder in terms of the age where they expect to excel and the demands that the coaches put on them. I think it's mentally difficult and one of the most physically demanding sports.
>
> (HBO, 2019, 5:15)

Many advice-oriented texts point to reasonable suggestions like not pushing your child too hard, not comparing them to other athletes, not trying to coach them from the stands, and not focusing too much on scores—all with the goal of promoting a gymnast's success. Yet far fewer of these texts emphasize a parent's responsibility in ensuring their gymnast's *welfare,* such as looking for signs of excessive stress or depression, monitoring repeated injuries, watching for signs of an eating disorder, asking questions about training safety, and insisting on being present when their gymnast is alone with another adult. There is an assumption that a gymnast will get hurt and a parent must accept this risk without questioning the coach's training techniques or safety practices. One study found that 40 percent of gymnasts ages 6–10 regularly suffer from tendonitis and that 83 percent of the top European junior gymnasts had abnormalities of the radial bones in their arms (Personne, 1995, as cited in Kerr, 2014). In *At the Heart of Gold,* Dawn Homer, mother of former gymnast Trinea Gonczar, describes her experience as a gymnastics mom and her daughter's training:

> It did not matter what happened to [her daughter]. You were not to cry. There were things like when they would be racked. Racking is just like a torture to these girls. It's just trying to force them down into splits, and you've got such adult pressure being put on these little girls. And they are not to cry. They are not to yell out. But yet you know they are in so much pain. But they just do it, without complaint.
>
> (HBO, 2019, 5:34)

In addition to the haunting visual, Homer keys in on an ethical tension in athletic training: the expectation that children will act like adults (without tears or complaints). Personally, I have also seen children face consequences based on their coaches' adult expectations, sometimes for infractions that are not within their control. For example, when my daughter trains at her gym, she and her fellow gymnasts must climb a rope dozens of feet into the air as "punishment" for being late to practice, even though none of the girls are old enough to drive and manage their own schedules. Similar consequences for tardiness are not uncommon in other youth sports, and on the surface, they have a noble goal of promoting timeliness and responsibility. But ethically, personal accountability cannot be void of individual agency.

I see issues like the intentional separation of parents from their children and adult expectations placed on minors in athletic training as only two symptoms of what I will call a "rhetorical culture of champion-building." Other characteristics of this culture include using fear and shame to motivate, maintain order, and ultimately silence; separating the athlete from their tool (body) and ability (skill); and normalizing pain and a high risk of (often repeated) injury. Peter Donnelly (1997) writes about the risk of injury in youth sport:

> In no other occupation or profession, even for adults, would the high rate of burnout, the high rate of overuse injuries, the serious potential for traumatic injury, [and] the serious possibility of long-term disability (i.e. arthritis or growth-plate damage),... be allowed to pass without question.
>
> (p. 394)

I suggest that fear-based and shame-based instructional techniques, particularly as related to the body and power differentials, also actively discourage or even prevent athletes from speaking up about abuse and important concerns about their welfare. Speaking up for oneself is hindered by "rhetorical cultures of champion-building." In elite programs, "coachable" athletes are the goal, and often "coachable" translates into the athlete who does not complain or show discomfort. In highly competitive programs, the consequences of speaking up—even for perfectly reasonable purposes—may mean getting cut from the program and being replaced by other more "coachable" athletes. This culture continuously reinforces the "disposability" of athletes in lieu of acknowledging athletes' concerns and taking appropriate action to protect their wellbeing.

Coincidentally, based on new guidelines issued by USA Gymnastics in the wake of the Nassar scandal, my daughter's gym has changed their policies to allow parents to observe any practice at any time. But in this case, it was not because of anything I or any of my fellow gym parents said. Changes were enacted in the sport as a whole because other parents and athletes chose to speak up, unfortunately after the unimaginable happened to them.

Objectives of this book

When Simone Biles withdrew from the gymnastics team finals at the Tokyo Olympics in 2021 to focus on her mental health, she drew both criticism and praise for prioritizing her own wellbeing over the team competition. She also drew worldwide attention to the issue of mental health and athletics—certainly not a new conversation, but one that has lived in the shadows of a sports culture that demands greater-than-human perfection from its hero-athletes. Some sports brands quickly latched onto the issue of athlete mental health as part of their marketing strategies. Within months, Nike launched a new "Nike Mind Sets" program that focuses on prioritizing athletes' mental health and wellbeing over achievement (Bleier, 2021). In March 2022, Powerade launched a global ad campaign, starring Biles alongside other high-profile athletes, featuring the slogan "Pause is Power." The debut ad encourages giving athletes "time to be human" and celebrates "the regenerative strength that can be found in a moment of pause" from training and competition (Jardine, 2022). Champion tennis player Naomi Osaka, NFL star Calvin Ridley, former NBA Rookie of the Year Ben Simmons, and other athletes have also been speaking out about their own challenges with mental health in professional sports (Bleier, 2021).

In the mental health field, studies have addressed the toxicity of sport culture on athletes' mental health, from depression, anxiety, and suicide to eating disorders and substance abuse (e.g., Brown, 2014; Brown & Blanton, 2002; Etzel et al., 2006). In the spring of 2022 alone, at least five NCAA athletes died by suicide, prompting calls for the NCAA to better support its athletes' mental health and prioritize young people over wins and profits (Hensley-Clancy, 2022). The "rhetoric of champion-building" suggests a necessary separation of mind and body (i.e., ignore pain or other signals of the mind to push the body further) that has physical and emotional consequences in athletes. In these situations, speaking up to report abuse, injury, burnout, or other issues may actually be more harmful than beneficial to the victim. While many factors contribute to an athlete's overall mental and physical health, this book highlights how the reluctance to report abuse and other issues is specifically a problem of rhetoric and communication—of speaking up and silencing.

In particular, on college campuses, we have seen a wave of recent abuse scandals in the news involving coaching staff and team physicians who abused student-athletes for decades without consequence. As in other organizations, under-reporting of sexual violence on college campuses is an issue, though the exact figures vary. One U.S. Department of Justice report estimates that more than 90 percent of women who are victims of sexual assault on college campuses do not report the assault (Fisher et al., 2000). And even if cases are reported, they may not lead to action or effective results. Title IX of the Education Amendments Act of 1972 is the federal legislation that prohibits sexual discrimination in educational institutions. Sexual harassment—which includes acts of sexual violence such as rape, sexual battery, and sexual coercion—is a form of gender-based discrimination prohibited by Title IX. Tara Richards' 2019 study of data from Annual Security Reports (ASRs) and Title IX Coordinators found that ASRs undercounted incidents of sexual misconduct, few incidents reported to Title IX Coordinators resulted in formal Title IX complaints, and even fewer resulted in a finding of responsibility or suspension/expulsion of the accused (p. 180).

In these statistics, I see multifaceted problems of speaking, silencing, and listening in organizations that should prompt further investigation of cultures of abuse and organizational practices that silence victims while protecting abusers. I therefore focus this book on two main research questions to explore the relationship between organization, violence, and silence in youth and college sports programs. First, I ask if systems and rhetorics of silencing are embedded in youth and intercollegiate athletics organizations, and, if so, what impact do they have on athletes? I then examine how the rhetoric and discursive practices of youth and college athletic programs impact athletes' willingness to speak up about abuse.

This book focuses on the specific case study of the Larry Nassar abuse scandal at Michigan State University and within USA Gymnastics. The question of how organizations like USA Gymnastics and Michigan State University could so tragically fail to protect their athletes still very much remains a gap in our current knowledge. If athletes are under extreme pressure not to speak up about any issues, then by design, Title IX may be ineffective and even counterproductive. Title IX may be another piece in a collective, flawed organizational process that serves to silence student-athletes while preserving above all else the organization and its reputation (Doyle, 2015, p. 69). Rhetorical analysis (defined here as the study of how words, images, and discursive practices are used to influence audiences), and in particular concepts of rhetorical silence and silencing, play a key role in this research. To better describe the rhetorical cultures that underpin this book's objectives and the exigency of this research in the field, it is first necessary to consider two related areas: (1) sexual violence and athletics and (2) silence and silencing in youth and college athletics.

Sexual violence and athletics

Larry Nassar (Michigan State), Jerry Sandusky (Penn State), Richard Strauss (Ohio State), and now Robert Anderson (University of Michigan)—mentioning just a few names from recent headlines suggests that there is a problem of both speaking up about abuse and listening to victims of abuse in college athletic programs. Former USA Gymnastics and Michigan State University doctor Larry Nassar was sentenced to 140–360 years in prison during state and federal trials in 2017 and 2018 for sexual abuse of women and girls that went unreported for decades and impacted hundreds of victims (Vaidyanathan, 2018). In 2011, Pennsylvania State University assistant coach Jerry Sandusky was arrested and charged with 52 counts of sexual abuse of young boys from 1994 to 2009 (Viera, 2011). Sandusky had strategically abused boys he met through his non-profit organization for at-risk youth for 15 years before facing criminal charges. Former Ohio State team doctor

Richard Strauss has been accused of sexually abusing hundreds of men and boys over a 20-year period (Buduson, 2021). In January 2022, the University of Michigan reached a settlement with more than 1,000 victims who have accused former university physician Robert Anderson of sexual assault that spanned more than 30 years (Vitagliano, 2022). Strauss died in 2005, and Anderson died in 2008. Neither faced prosecution for their crimes.

In the wake of these cases and others, many might ask how a sexual predator could get away with these crimes for so long. Why was nothing reported? Why did nobody speak up? Why was nobody held accountable? Why weren't safeguards in place to protect athletes? In all four examples above, the organizations had at least some knowledge of the abuse or complaints years before the cases caught public attention, but the organizations took little to no action against the abusers. And for every victim report that was ignored or downplayed, hundreds went unreported.

Sexual violence is considered a form of sexual harassment prohibited in educational institutions under Title IX of the Education Amendments Act of 1972. According to the U.S. Department of Education's Office for Civil Rights, sexual harassment is any unwelcome conduct of a sexual nature, such as unwelcome sexual advances; requests for sexual favors; and other verbal, nonverbal, or physical conduct of a sexual nature. Sexual violence is physical sexual acts perpetrated against a person's will or when a person is incapable of giving consent. Examples include rape, sexual assault, sexual battery, sexual coercion, unwanted touching, dating violence, and stalking.

One important question in studying sexual violence and athletics is the relationship between gender and violence/silence. Is sexual assault a gendered form of violence? "Violence" and "silence" are both often perceived as gendered terms—as masculine and feminine, respectively. Jennifer Doyle (2015) argues that master narratives are always sexist (and racist), and therefore the popular imagination of sexual violence on campus is the risk of the "young girl" being violated by the "non-affiliate" man (i.e., the outsider who should not be on campus). Writing about the rhetorical potential of silence, Cheryl Glenn (2004) constructs silence as a traditionally feminine site, whereas speaking, signaling power, is masculine. I recognize the complex theoretical question of gender and its relationship to any study of power, silence, and violence. However, people anywhere on the gender spectrum can be victims of sexual harassment or sexual violence. For example, three of my four opening examples (all but Nassar) involved abuse of men and boys. Since I was drawn to this research by my experiences with my daughter, and I am particularly interested in how the "rhetorical culture of champion-building" impacted victims of Larry Nassar's sexual assault, my focus is specifically on the abuse of gymnasts who are women. However, additional studies should continue to examine important issues related to gender and athletic training, like whether women student-athletes are less likely to self-report abuse than men and the prevalence of violence against transgender student-athletes.

Another important problem is the potential impact of fear-based training on athletes' willingness to speak up about abuse. We know that athletic coaching is often fear based. All instruction does, to some degree, involve an element of fear. Students fear failing, disappointing themselves and others, wasting time and money, missing opportunities, etc. I suggest that speaking up for oneself is often actively discouraged in athletic programs, as reflected in phrases and slogans connected with what I have called "rhetorical cultures of champion-building:" Do as you're told. Don't show emotions. Suck it up. Be a champion. Just do it. "That's the whole thing about being a great gymnast," says Olympic gymnast Kathy Johnson in *At the Heart of Gold.* "It's almost like being a wounded animal. You don't show your weakness. You don't show that you're hurt" (HBO, 2019, 6:29). The pressure to remain silent and "push through" any personal or bodily discomfort may be so ingrained in the cultural fabric of athletic training—in the habituated daily experience of athletes—that speaking up, even about abuse, does not ever seem like a reasonable option. In *At the Heart of Gold,* Jessica O'Beirne, a journalist who covered the Larry Nassar case, laments that "gymnastics is not a sport with a lot of back-and-forth communication. It's a lot of... soldier, learning how to be a soldier" (HBO, 2019, 6:43). Gymnasts are taught, at every practice and every meet, to fall in line without a word. Again, I find in this research a problem of communication, a problem of speaking up and silencing.

One challenge I encountered in this study is that few scholars in communication or rhetoric are specifically studying athletic training. Scholars have addressed sports broadly, including topics of gender/sexuality/identity in sports, sports fandom, and media representation. However, research on abuse and assault in sport is relatively new in any field, with athlete rights discourses only appearing very recently (Brackenridge, 2014). Considerable research has documented sexual violence and harassment on U.S. college campuses, including studies of where and how assault occurs, where and how it is reported (if reported), how it is adjudicated, and various models to combat sexual violence (Burnett et al., 2009; Conrad & Taylor, 1994; Dunn, 2013; Engle, 2015; Fisher & Sloan, 2007; Hartmann, 2015; Hayes-Smith & Levett, 2010; Koss et al., 2014; Krebs et al., 2007; Lombardi & Jones, 2009; Sable et al., 2006; Schwilk et al., 2017; Shafer, 2007; Weizel, 2012). These studies come from a variety of fields, including communication, gender studies, law, criminology, psychology and mental health, college health, and education.

As will be discussed later in the book, warnings about a culture of abuse in women's gymnastics had sounded long before Larry Nassar's name hit global headlines. Perhaps most notably, in 1995, journalist Joan Ryan first published her book *Little Girls in Pretty Boxes,* a scathing exposé of the training conditions endured by elite gymnasts and figure skaters. While her focus is not specifically sexual abuse, Ryan chronicles a training culture of frequent injuries, eating disorders, unrealistic image expectations, unrelenting pressure, politics and money, and cutthroat coaching that demands absolute subservience and adult responsibilities from child athletes who have none of the rights of adults (Ryan, 1995). A subsequent article published in *The New England Journal of Medicine* likewise warned about the physical and emotional consequences of elite female gymnastics training that put athletes at risk for abuse (Tofler et al., 1996). Again, though the focus was not specifically on sexual abuse, the danger to athletes trained using such techniques was clear.

To date, when researchers have focused primarily on the relationship between campus sexual violence/harassment and athletes, it has been to document the prevalence of violence among student-athletes and a potential rape culture in college athletic programs (e.g., McCray, 2015). For example, in *Unsportsmanlike Conduct: College Football and the Politics of Rape,* Jessica Luther (2016) investigates "the intersection of college football and sexual assault, and the people and systems that ignore, minimize, and even perpetuate this violence" (p. 24). Dave Zirin declares in the editor's foreword to Luther's book that "our college campuses have a sexual assault problem," citing startling statistics like one in five women have faced sexual violence on campus and 80 percent of all cases of campus sexual assault go unreported (p. 16). Luther, who has a journalism background, studies high-profile examples like Jameis Winston's sexual assault case at Florida State University to argue that institutions—from athletic departments, to the press, to the NCAA—perpetually run the same "plays" to effectively sweep sexual assault cases under the institutional rug (2016).

While such research is valuable in revealing troubling trends and the failure of universities to protect victims, much less focus has centered on student-athletes as potential victims of sexual crimes and systems of silencing and inequality that perpetuate abuse. In other words, researchers tend to investigate whether a football player is more likely to commit a sexual crime rather than whether a gymnast is less likely to report an assault than non-athletic students. Further critical study and empirical research on the experiences of athletes in youth and college-level sports programs are warranted, particularly as they relate to violence and silence. Recent highly visible events in the sports world have put a much more intense spotlight on issues of athletes' rights and mental health, making it a particularly appropriate time for the fields of rhetoric and communication to contribute to the dialogue.

Silence and silencing in youth and college athletics

Silence is more than the absence of sound. Silence can be a rhetoric. In "Silence: A Rhetorical Art for Resisting Discipline(s)," Cheryl Glenn writes:

> Silence and silencing both resist the traditional discipline of rhetoric—at the same time that they work to transform it. The transformative power of silence isn't obvious; that is, it's not obvious if rhetoric can only be delivered by words and if rhetoric can only be about establishing power. But when the delivery of purposeful silence is considered a strategic choice, its presence resonates with meaning and intention—just like that of the spoken word.
>
> (p. 282)

Embracing silence as a rhetoric does mean resisting traditional concepts of rhetoric and its purpose. It is therefore important here to put forth a definition of "rhetoric" and its goals. Aristotle famously defined rhetoric as the "available means of persuasion," which, along with the five classical canons of rhetoric (invention, arrangement, style, memory, and delivery), served as the center of Western education in rhetoric until at least the mid-20th century to train speakers and writers to effectively persuade their audiences. Rhetoric's relation to ethics has transformed over the past 60–70 years from our Aristotelian/Platonic/Socratic inheritance to the introduction of multiple new perspectives and voices, including an increasing focus on ethical concerns and rhetorical goals beyond persuasion. Scholars like Lisbeth Lipari (2012) and Krista Ratcliffe (2005), for example, suggest a "turn" within our discipline from "confrontational" rhetoric to "invitational" rhetoric and techniques of rhetorical listening. Confrontational rhetoric—more in line with rhetoric grounded in traditional Western and/or European institutions and attitudes—seeks to persuade, conquer, convert, and ultimately change others. Robert Connors calls this instruction in persuasive public discourse "agonistic rhetoric," which he argues largely characterized the education of men until 1850 (Lauer, 1995, p. 276). Invitational rhetoric was originally defined by feminist scholars Sonja Foss and Cindy Griffin (1995) as "an invitation to understanding as a means to create a relationship rooted in equality, immanent value, and self-determination" (p. 5). In contrast to rhetoric as a means of persuasion, rhetorical listening is defined by Ratcliffe as "a stance of openness that a person may choose to assume in relation to any person, text, or culture" (2005, p. 1). I embrace invitational rhetoric, most importantly because it opens the possibility of rhetorical listening that, as Glenn notes, leads to the possibility of understanding (2002).

In theorizing the relationship between speech and silence as reciprocal rather than oppositional, Glenn resists traditional concepts of rhetoric that privilege words over silence, speaking over listening, and persuasion over understanding. In fact, as a rhetorical art, silence has many rhetorical meanings and uses. Based on communication research, Richard Johannesen developed a list of no fewer than 20 potential meanings for silence, from reflecting anger or rudeness, to expressing agreement or disagreement, to enhancing the silent one's own isolation or independence (Glenn, 2004, p. 16). Johannesen's list of meanings for silence synthesizes the work of communication scholars Hugh Duncan, Paul Goodman, Alice Greene, Karl Jaspers, Joseph Lebo, Joost Meerloo, Robert Oliver, Walter Ong, Robert Scott, and Geoffrey Wagner (Glenn, 2004, p. 166). As mentioned, silence can open a space for rhetorical listening and attentiveness. Silence can be a form of protest or resistance; it can be the refusal to speak. In educational settings, silence can establish an orderly setting for teaching and learning or, as in my current case, silence can open a space to think and write about a research project. Silence can be used for religious practices, contemplation, meditation, self-improvement, and prayer (Glenn, 2004,

p. 18). But silence is not always empowering or voluntary. Silence can be a form of punishment, a means of obedience or subordination, or a consequence of fear and powerlessness.

As noted before, silence was responsible for drawing me to this research topic. As a mother of athletic children, I have been thrust into the before unknown (to me) world of youth athletic training, including my daughter's experiences a member of a compulsory gymnastics team. ("Compulsory" refers to Levels 1–5 in the USA Gymnastics Junior Olympic Program.) We have known there is a problem in the world with silencing vulnerable populations, perhaps even before Spivak asked if the subaltern could speak at all (Spivak, 1994). My research project identifies youth and college-level athletes as a potentially vulnerable population, and one of my research questions is whether the rhetoric and discursive practices of youth and college athletic programs impact athletes' willingness to speak up about abuse. Glenn finds power in purposeful silence as a strategic choice. But she also points out in *Unspoken* that silence by choice functions differently from silence enforced by others (2004, p. 14). Silence can both give power and be the absence of power. One question I had to grapple with in this research, then, was the relationship between power and silence and whether the "decision" to speak up or remain silent in the cases studied was always truly a choice. Robert Scott writes about the motivations for silence that "every decision to say something is a decision not to say something else, that is, if the utterance is a *choice*. In speaking we remain silent. And in remaining silent, we speak" (1972, p. 146). *Choice* is a significant word here. In fear-based and shame-based situations of physical and mental abuse, I question whether speaking out is always a choice at one's disposal.

My research into the Larry Nassar abuse scandal at Michigan State University and within USA Gymnastics involved reading and analyzing victims' statements, stories, and testimonies. In these cases, under various personal and public pressures, victims have "chosen" to speak out. Still, it has become clear to me from these narratives that, before words could come, silence was about survival for a person stripped of power. For example, *After Silence* is Nancy Raine's story of being raped by a stranger in her home and the 7 years of personal silence, struggles with powerlessness, and feelings of isolation that followed. While Raine was not an athlete, I find her story particularly relevant (and moving) in relation to this study, in part because she specifically addresses her motivation to speak up. Partly, her choice to speak was stripped away by fear and shame. Her rapist repeatedly told her to "shut up" during the attack; for 7 years after, she continued to comply. Yet she also points to a silencing from those around her, even close family, who were uncomfortable speaking of the rape and hoped that she would forget. The silence of survivors, Raine argues, is "supported by a profound collective anxiety about rape that borders on cultural psychosis" (1998, p. 5). Rape has historically been considered a crime "so unspeakable, so shameful to its victims" that they are "rendered mute and cloaked in protective anonymity" (1998, p. 6). Jennifer Doyle makes a similar argument (though about a different case) of universities' inability to talk about words like "rape" and "sodomy" as though allowing such words to enter into conversation violates a social contract of congenial dialogue (2015, p. 75). In *Sexual Violence in Western Thought and Writing: Chaste Rape,* Victor Vitanza (2011) writes that "no act against another is more devastating than rape (sexual violence); no act is more impossible to think, read, write than rape" (p. xii). Vitanza suggests that the problem of "chasteness" in sexual violence, which makes rape hidden and silenced from public discussion, is that rape narratives and sexual violence are not necessarily hidden at all but are in fact part of both the foundation of Western culture and of everyday life. Vitanza writes, "After numerous dosages of repetitious exemplars of founding rape scripts and narratives as well as daily rapes, we become immune and, consequently, build up a resistance to them. In the political unconscious. They become, yet incipiently remain, Chaste Rapes" (p. xiv). Rape is therefore unthinkable, unspeakable because it is hidden superficially, and chastely, on the surface (p. xx).

Raine ultimately chooses to make rape less "unspeakable" by giving language to her experiences—by speaking up. Her story suggests that one potential "use" of rhetorical silence in situations of abuse is actually breaking it, in regaining power through words and testimony. Adrienne Rich (1979) echoes this dynamic between power and speaking truth:

> If we have learned anything in our coming out of silence, it is that what has been unspoken, therefore *unspeakable* in us, is what is most threatening to the patriarchal order in which some men control, first women, then all who can be defined and exploited as "other."
>
> (p. 199)

Perhaps giving voice/paying attention to silence and talking publicly about assault and abuse is an important kind of resistance.

The choice to speak is further confounded when silencing comes at the institutional level. Communication professor Robin Patric Clair (1998) writes extensively about what she terms "silencing communication" and how language, society, and organizations support and reproduce forms of silencing. She argues that silence is both a product of sexual violence and a means of perpetuating systems of assault. Victims rarely go through formal channels to make sexual harassment complaints because they expect their claims to be ignored or trivialized to protect established dominant structures, and victims also have no guarantee of protection from harassment or retaliation (1998, p. 77). The result, therefore, is avoidance and silence.

In her 1993 study of sexual harassment at the Big Ten universities, Clair examines how sexual harassment can be a "discursive practice that can be enacted, tolerated, perpetuated, or rectified through communication" (p. 123). Based on her textual analysis of policies and brochures produced by Big Ten universities, Clair concludes that this discourse contributes to the "commodification, bureaucratization, and privatization" of sexual harassment (p. 123). The result is institutionalized discourse that marginalizes victims, usually women and minorities; reproduces systems of harassment; and perpetuates patriarchal practices (Clair, 1993).

The fields of psychology and sociology have described a "secondary assault" to victims of trauma when the institutions charged with protecting them and adjudicating their cases fail them. Psychologists Carly Parnitzke Smith and Jennifer Freyd (2014) describe this concept as "institutional betrayal," which occurs when trusted and powerful institutions like universities, churches, and government organizations act "in ways that visit harm upon those dependent on them for safety and well-being" (p. 575). A college student who reports a sexual assault, for example, might then experience institutional harassment or callous investigative practices that further the student's trauma. Institutional betrayal also occurs when institutional systems and cultures foster abuse and protect abusers, and when institutions put reputations and profits before the wellbeing of their members. Smith and Freyd argue that, in cases of abuse and assault, institutions have "the potential to either worsen posttraumatic outcomes or become sources of justice, support, and healing" (2014, p. 576). The question of institutional support of and responses to silencing inevitably surfaced in this research, as I explored how organization and silence are related.

Within the context of the Larry Nassar scandal, I investigated what systems and rhetorics of silencing are embedded in intercollegiate athletics organizations and what impact these systems of silencing might have on student-athletes. I also analyzed the failure of Michigan State University, USA Gymnastics, the U.S. Olympic and Paralympic Committee, and other organizations connected to Larry Nassar to protect athletes, including athletes who did come forward with complaints against Nassar.

In terms of institutional response, speaking up seems to often be connected to media inquiry—leading to the moment when the silence is broken and the secret is finally forced out by public attention. As mentioned, in the cases of Nassar (Michigan State), Sandusky (Penn State), Strauss (Ohio State), and Anderson (University of Michigan), the organizations had at least some knowledge of the abuse or complaints years before the cases caught public attention, but the organizations took little to no action against the abusers. Doyle chronicles a number of cases of campus violence that were swept under the institutional rug until media headlines and the ensuing publicity forced action, including the violent arrest of Dr. Ersula Ore, a professor at Arizona State University (ASU), for jaywalking (2015, p. 102). Ore (2015) describes her confrontation with officers and subsequent arrest in *Present Tense*. While crossing a street on her way home after teaching class, Ore was stopped by an ASU police officer and asked, without an apparent reason, to show her ID. When she refused and questioned the officer's actions, Ore was aggressively handcuffed and arrested. When the patrol car's dash cam video was later aired by local news more than a month later, it went viral, prompting outrage and ultimately a response from ASU. For cases like Ore's and others, further research may suggest that the press has a rhetorical exigence in interrupting institutional silence.

Another thread I investigate in this research is the efficacy of Title IX as the *institutional* means for reporting and investigating incidents of sexual discrimination, including sexual harassment and sexual violence, on college campuses. It is important to investigate Title IX legislation in its current form and whether systems are in place to protect athletes and encourage them to speak up. One Detroit news investigation found that recent Title IX investigations at Michigan State University took as long as a year to conclude, with 10 percent of cases filed in 2019 taking more than 200 days, and suggested that lengthy and complicated Title IX processes can cause further trauma to victims (Jones, 2020). As another illustration, in January 2020, the United States Sixth Circuit Court of Appeals affirmed a lower court's dismissal of a lawsuit filed by student-athletes against a football coach in the St. Mary's City School District (Ohio) who consistently used obscene language and derogatory terms like "pussy," "bitch," and "pretty boy" to "motivate his student-athletes to be 'tough'" (Grate, 2020). Though an investigation by the school district confirmed the students' allegations, the district ultimately decided that the coach's behavior was not inappropriate, so the plaintiffs then filed a lawsuit under Title IX (Grate, 2020). Though the Sixth Circuit's majority opinion did not endorse the use of derogatory terms, they concluded that crude or vulgar language does not violate Title IX and that the "coach's conduct did not satisfy the high bar of establishing infliction of emotional distress" (Grate, 2020). In other words, swearing at a student and calling him a "pussy" is a permissible way to motivate a student-athlete under Title IX. So, I must ask, is this language also permissible for other educators? May an English teacher, for example, use the same language to motivate students to write better papers? Do we, perhaps, impose a different standard for coaches and student-athletes?

This topic came to me as a "felt issue," as a mother whose experiences had raised concerns about her children's participation in athletic programs. I know the silencing power of fear, and it is a motivating factor in this research. As a professor, I have taught classes composed almost exclusively of student-athletes. (In some cases, more than 90 percent of the students in my classes were also athletes.) In the classroom, I often sensed my students' hesitation to speak up or to challenge authority. Anecdotally, when teaching about tone and goodwill in professional writing to these classes, I was surprised by the number of my students who did not understand why a writer should make an intentional effort to craft their messages in a positive and forward-looking way. They valued straightforwardness, but they also did not question excessive negativity. It made me wonder, what messages were these students used to receiving?

I think it is important to note, therefore, that I write from the perspective of a participant and with a purpose and goals that are at the same time both universal and quite personal. I am a "sports parent" and a teacher to student-athletes, but I also happen to be a trained rhetorician and professional communicator. I have an investment in both worlds, and one of my hopes in this research is drawing attention to the potential collaboration between those who study, teach, and play athletics with scholars in communication, rhetoric, and writing studies to analyze problems connected to abuse and prompt change. And unfortunately, we have an ever-growing number of cases to study.

With the emergence of the #MeToo movement, spotlight on the tragic USA Gymnastics scandal, and global rise in activism against sexual violence, such a study has a particularly *kairotic* purpose and moment within the disciplines of rhetoric and communication. These disciplines are especially well-suited to investigate the rhetorical cultures, ideologies, and systems of power and abuse at the heart of these issues. Rhetorical analysis, in particular, is an appropriate lens to evaluate and interrogate cultures and institutions, in this case USA Gymnastics and Michigan State University, where language, habits, and ideologies are acquired, reproduced, and embedded and the ultimate impact on individuals.

With origins in design thinking, the "wicked problems" approach to solving problems that do not have straightforward solutions was formulated by Horst Rittel in the 1960s (Buchanan, 1992). In tackling large-scale issues of social change, like environmental protection and gender discrimination, communicators and rhetoricians often face wicked problems that cannot be solved with a single, linear solution. Chad Wickman (2014) argues for a wicked problems approach in teaching technical communication that "grounds conceptual learning in practical experience and real-world scenarios" while engaging students with "issues that have no immediate or single solution yet demand an immediate and singular response" (p. 25). I want to be clear that I consider the problem of abuse in youth and college athletics to be a *wicked* problem that cannot be solved by one person or one study. The bigger picture of what meaningful change for athletes means is daunting, really. I see lasting change only prompted by a global movement spurred by different voices from many disciplines transforming many different areas, from policy and procedural changes to everyday interactions between athletes, parents/guardians, and coaching staff. Protecting athletes would mean cultural shifts in athletic training, as well as social constructs of "the athlete." So, we must tackle this urgent, wicked problem one solution at a time.

References

Bleier, E. (2021, November 19). Nike's new mind sets program will focus on mental, not physical, health. *InsideHook*. Retrieved from https://www. insidehook.com/daily_brief/sports/nikes-mind-sets-program-focus-mental-health

Brackenridge, C. H. (2014). Setting the challenge: The ethical and research context of children's involvement in elite sport. In C. H. Brackenridge, & D. Rhind (Eds.), *Elite child athlete welfare* (pp. 13–19). London: Brunel University Press.

Brown, D., & Blanton, C. (2002). Physical activity, sports participation, and suicidal behavior among college students. *Medicine & Science in Sports and Exercise*, 34(7), 1087–1096.

Brown, G. T. (Ed.) (2014). *Mind, body and sport: Understanding and supporting student-athlete mental wellness.* Indianapolis, IN: National Collegiate Athletic Association.

Brown, M. (2017). Words across the waters. *Tales of the 10th West Irregulars.* Retrieved from https://10thwestirregulars.blogspot.com/2017/07/words-across-water.html

Buchanan, R. (1992). Wicked problems in design thinking. *Design Issues*, 8(2), 5–21.

Buduson, S. (2021, September 3). Betrayed: How Ohio failed hundreds of male athletes abused by OSU's Dr. Richard Strauss. *News 5 Cleveland.* Retrieved from https://www.news5cleveland.com/news/local-news/investigations/betrayed-how-ohio-failed-hundreds-of-male-athletes-abused-by-osus-dr-richard-strauss

Burnett, A., Mattern, J. L., Herakova, L. L., Kahl, D. H., Tobola, C., & Bornsen, S. E. (2009). Communicating/muting date rape: A co-cultural theoretical analysis of communication factors related to rape culture on a college campus. *Journal of Applied Communication Research*, 37(4), 465–485.

Clair, R. P. (1993). The bureaucratization, commodification, and privatization of sexual harassment through institutional discourse: A study of the big ten universities. *Management Communication Quarterly*, 7(2), 123–157.

Clair, R. P. (1998). *Organizing silence: A world of possibilities.* Albany, NY: SUNY.

Conrad, C., & Taylor, B. (1994). The context(s) of sexual harassment: Power, silences, and academe. In S. G. Bingham (Ed.), *Conceptualizing sexual harassment as discursive practice* (pp. 45–58). Westport, CT: Praeger.

Donnelly, P. (1997). Child labour, sport labour: Applying child labour laws to sport. *International Review for the Sociology of Sport*, 32(4), 389–406.

Doyle, J. (2015). *Campus sex, campus security.* South Pasadena, CA: Semiotext(e).

Dunn, L. L. (2013). Addressing sexual violence in higher education: Ensuring compliance with the Clery Act, Title IX and VAWA. *The Georgetown Journal of Gender & Law,* 15, 563–584.

Engle, J. C. (2015). Mandatory reporting of campus sexual assault and domestic violence: Moving to a victim-centric protocol that comports with federal law. *Temple Political and Civil Rights Law Review,* 24(2), 401–421.

Etzel, E. F., Watson, J. C., Visek, A. J., & Maniar, S. D. (2006). Understanding and promoting college student-athlete health: Essential issues for student affairs professionals. *NASPA Journal,* 43(3), 518–546.

Fisher, B., Cullen, F., & Turner, M. (2000). *The sexual victimization of college women.* Retrieved from https://www.ncjrs.gov/pdffiles1/nij/182369.pdf

Fisher, B. S., & Sloan, J. J. (Eds.) (2007). *Campus crime: Legal, social, and policy perspectives.* Springfield, IL: Charles C. Thomas.

Foss, S., & Griffin, C. (1995). Beyond persuasion: A proposal for an invitational rhetoric. *Communication Monographs,* 62(1), 2–18.

Glenn, C. (2002). Silence: A rhetorical art for resisting discipline(s). *JAC,* 22(2), 261–291.

Glenn, C. (2004). *Unspoken: A rhetoric of silence.* Carbondale, IL: Southern Illinois University Press.

Grate, M. (2020, January 21). Use of derogatory terms to motivate student-athletes is permissible under Title IX. *JD Supra.* Retrieved from https://www.jdsupra.com/legalnews/use-of-derogatory-terms-to-motivate-92131/

Hartmann, A. (2015). Reworking sexual assault response on university campuses: Creating a rights-based empowerment model to minimize institutional liability. *Washington University Journal of Law & Policy,* 48, 287–320.

Hayes-Smith, R. M., & Levett, L. M. (2010). Student perceptions of sexual assault resources and prevalence of rape myth attitudes. *Feminist Criminology,* 5(4), 335–354.

Hensley-Clancy, M. (2022, May 20). Reeling from suicides, college athletes press NCAA: "This is a crisis." *The Washington Post.* Retrieved from https://www.washingtonpost.com/sports/2022/05/19/college-athletes-suicide-mental-health/

Jardine, A. (2022, March 14). Powerade focuses on the power of "pause" in mental health-focused ad with Simone Biles. *AdAge.* Retrieved from https://adage.com/article/marketing-news-strategy/powerade-debuts-mental-health-focused-ad-simone-biles/2405476

Jones, R. (2020, February 10). Lengthy Title IX investigations at MSU leave survivors retraumatized. *WXYZ Detroit.* Retrieved from https://www.wxyz.com/news/local-news/investigations/lengthy-title-ix-investigations-at-msu-leave-survivors-retraumatized

Kerr, G. (2014). Physical and emotional abuse of elite child athletes: The case of forced physical exertion. In C. H. Brackenridge, & D. Rhind

(Eds.), *Elite child athlete welfare* (pp. 41–50). London: Brunel University Press.

Koss, M. P., Wilgus, J., & Williams, K. M. (2014). Campus sexual misconduct: Restorative justice approaches to enhance compliance with Title IX guidance. *Trauma, Violence, and Abuse,* 15(3), 242–257.

Krebs, C. P., Lindquist, C. H., Warner, T. D., Fisher, B. S., & Martin, S. L. (2007). *The campus sexual assault (CSA) study* (NCJRS Document No. 221153). Retrieved from https://www.ncjrs.gov/pdffiles1/nij/grants/221153.pdf

Lauer, J. M. (1995). The feminization of rhetoric and composition studies. *Rhetoric Review,* 13(2), 276–286.

Lipari, L. (2012). Rhetoric's other: Levinas, listening, and the ethical response. *Philosophy and Rhetoric,* 45(3), 227–245.

Lombardi, K., & Jones, K. (2009). *Campus sexual assault statistics don't add up: The troubling discrepancies in Clery Act numbers.* Washington, DC: The Center for Public Integrity. Retrieved from https://publicintegrity.org/education/campus-sexual-assault-statistics-dont-add-up/

Luther, J. (2016). *Unsportsmanlike conduct: College football and the politics of rape.* Brooklyn, NY: Akashic Books.

McCray, K. L. (2015). Intercollegiate athletes and sexual violence: A review of literature and recommendations for future study. *Trauma, Violence, & Abuse,* 16(4), 438–443.

Ore, E. J. (2015). They call me Dr. Ore. *Present Tense,* 5(2). Retrieved from http://www.presenttensejournal.org/volume-5/they-call-me-dr-ore/

Raine, N. V. (1998). *After silence: Rape and my journey back.* New York: Three Rivers Press.

Ratcliffe, K. (2005). *Rhetorical listening: Identification, gender, whiteness.* Carbondale, IL: Southern Illinois University Press.

Rich, A. (1979). *On lies, secrets, and silence.* New York: Norton.

Richards, T. N. (2019). No evidence of "weaponized Title IX" here: An empirical assessment of sexual misconduct reporting, case processing, and outcomes. *Law and Human Behavior,* 43(2), 180–192.

Ryan, J. (1995). *Little girls in pretty boxes: The making and breaking of elite gymnasts and figure skaters.* New York: Doubleday.

Sable, M. R., Danis, F., Mauzy, D. L., & Gallagher, S. K. (2006). Barriers to reporting sexual assault for women and men: Perspectives of college students. *Journal of American College Health,* 55(3), 157–162.

Schwilk, C., Stevenson, R., & Bateman, D. (2017). *Sexual misconduct in the education and human services sector.* Hershey, PA: IGI Global.

Scott, R. L. (1972). Rhetoric and silence. *Western Speech Communication,* 36(3), 146–158.

Shafer, L. (2007). Women, gender, and safety on campus: Reporting is not enough. In B. S. Fisher, & J. J. Sloan (Eds.), *Campus crime: Legal, social, and policy perspectives* (pp. 87–101). Springfield, IL: Charles C. Thomas.

Smith, C. P., & Freyd, J. F. (2014). Institutional betrayal. *American Psychologist,* 69(6), 575–587.

Spivak, G. C. (1994). Can the subaltern speak? In P. Williams, & L. Chrisman (Eds.), *Colonial discourse and post-colonial theory: A reader* (pp. 66–111). New York: Columbia University Press.

Tofler, I. R., Stryer, B. K., Micheli, L. J., & Herman, L. R. (1996). Physical and emotional problems of elite female gymnasts. *The New England Journal of Medicine, 335*(4), 281–283.

"TOPS – Emeth Gymnastics." *Emeth Gymnastics.* Retrieved from https://emethgym.com/team/tops/

Ungerleider, S., & Ulich, D. (Producers), & Carr, E. L. (Director) (2019). *At the heart of gold: Inside the USA Gymnastics scandal* [Motion picture]. United States: HBO.

Vaidyanathan, R. (2018, January 25). Larry Nassar: Disgraced US Olympics doctor jailed for 175 years. *BBC News.* Retrieved from https://www.bbc.com/news/world-us-canada-42811304

Viera, M. (2011, November 5). Former coach at Penn State is charged with abuse. *The New York Times.* Retrieved from https://www.nytimes.com/2011/11/06/sports/ncaafootball/former-coach-at-penn-state-is-charged-with-abuse.html

Vitagliano, B. (2022, January 19). University of Michigan reaches $490 million settlement after sex abuse allegations against former UM doctor. *CNN.* Retrieved from https://www.cnn.com/2022/01/19/us/robert-anderson-university-of-michigan-settlement/index.html

Vitanza, V. J. (2011). *Sexual violence in western thought and writing: Chaste rape.* New York: Palgrave Macmillan.

Weizel, L. M. (2012). The process that is due: Preponderance of the evidence as the standard of proof for university adjudications of student-on-student sexual assault complaints. *Boston College Law Review, 53*(4), 1613–1655.

Wickman, C. (2014). Wicked problems in technical communication. *Journal of Technical Writing and Communication, 44*(1), 23–42.

2   Just do it
Rhetorical cultures of champion-building

I remember as a freshman undergraduate student, my fellow honors students and I were obliged to play a game called "Win All You Can" during orientation. This game is meant to be a team-building activity about trust, teamwork, and communication (though I recall it mostly led to hard feelings). After a quick online search, I found several possible iterations of this game, but essentially, your group is broken into teams and asked to make a series of two-option decisions. If all teams agree on the first option, you all win a certain amount of points. If teams disagree, some win and some lose points. The most profitable circumstance for an individual team is to convince all other teams to choose the first option, then double-cross them and choose the second option. Essentially, in the game of Win All You Can, agreement leads to consistent, modest gains for everyone. But double-crossing others, lying, and having no concern for other teams are actually the most lucrative strategies.

I refused to ever go against my word while playing and somehow convinced my teammates to take the moral high road, too. We lost miserably; we were dead last, in negative digits. Not long into the activity, my team discovered that this wasn't actually a game worth winning according to the established system of rewards, and we chose to do otherwise. I thought of this game as I considered the characteristics of a "rhetorical culture of champion-building." If a game can only be played to the highest level by sacrificing any concern for its players, is that game worth playing? Or do we need to reset the rules?

I have described a "rhetorical culture of champion-building" as using fear-based instructional techniques, particularly as related to the body and power differentials, that actively discourage or even prevent athletes from speaking up about abuse and important concerns about their welfare. Characteristics of this culture include

DOI: 10.4324/9781003349846-2

using fear and shame to motivate, maintain order, and ultimately silence; separating the athlete from their tool (body) and ability (skill); normalizing pain and a high risk of (often repeated) injury; and intentionally separating parents from their children in athletic training. In this chapter, I expand on these themes to further characterize the "rhetorical culture of champion-building" that serves as the scene of my case study and to consider how language, habits, and ideologies are acquired, reproduced, and embedded in athletic training.

Coachability

One of the most iconic scenes from the 1992 film *A League of Their Own* occurs when one of the all-women baseball players, Evelyn, makes a mistake during a game that costs the team their lead. Coach Jimmy Dugan screams violently into Evelyn's face after she makes the mistake, telling her to "start using your head, that's the lump that's three feet above your ass." When Evelyn begins to cry as a result, Jimmy declares incredulously: "There's no crying in baseball!" He recounts how his manager called him a "talking pile of pig shit" in front of his parents, but he didn't cry. Later, when Jimmy restrains himself while offering suggestions to Evelyn after she makes another mistake, the scene is intended purely for comedic effect. The viewer is meant to laugh at Jimmy's considerable effort (literally shaking with restraint) not to yell and cuss into the face of his player. The portrayal of this scene suggests that it is so unlikely for a baseball coach to consider and respect a player's emotional response and well-being while coaching, it is funny.

What does it mean for an athlete to be "coachable?" IMG Academy's (2019) article on "Teaching Your Child to be Coachable" suggests that one of the biggest challenges to coaches is athletes who are not open to coaching. Characteristics of the uncoachable athlete include feeling like they are never wrong, feeling they are being unfairly targeted by the coach, not taking responsibility for actions/mistakes, not taking criticism well, and being unwilling to learn. In an article written for PGA of America, Brandi Jackson (2017) offers six key ways for junior golfers to be more "coachable:" being willing to learn from more experienced players, respecting the coach, checking your ego at the door, practicing what your coach tells you to (even if you don't want to), accepting criticism, and being gracious and humble. While teaching a child to do things like taking criticism well and listening to their coach seem like perfectly reasonable goals, I suggest that the line between "disrespecting" a coach and standing up for personal concerns and appropriate physical/mental boundaries is not always clear-cut in the coach–athlete relationship. This is particularly true when coaching children, who are less likely to challenge authority and who lack the rhetorical agency of adults.

Located in Bradenton, Florida, IMG Academy bills itself as "the world's most prestigious sports, performance, and educational institution" and offers both a boarding school and sports camps. Studying and training at IMG Academy is cost-prohibitive for most families, with yearly tuition for most programs reaching more than $80,000. Since their goal is training for collegiate, professional, and Olympic-level athletes, I see IMG Academy's training advice on coachability as reflecting coaching values for elite-level training. In the same article about "Teaching Your Child to be Coachable," alongside suggestions like encouraging enthusiasm for learning and instilling a desire for growth, the writer also suggests that parents should not believe their children and actually advises parents to "avoid the instinct" to take their child's side against their coach. If the coach is yelling at your child, according to IMG Academy, a parent should allow their child to be "corrected" for their own good. "Rather than being upset with their coach for 'yelling' at them," says the article, "suggest to your child that they should be grateful that they have someone who wants them to improve and to become a better athlete." In time, the child will then "learn to adjust their attitude from one of resentment to one of gratitude." For IMG Academy, the key to the "coachable" athlete appears to be unquestioned respect for authority figures, a trait they suggest good athletes will then take into the workforce, noting that "un-coachable kids become unemployable adults."

Since the "coachable" athlete must trust and respect the coach without question (and parents are often asked to do the same), one important concern related to "coachability" is whether a coach always has a player's best interests in mind and is fostering a safe training environment. IMG Academy's article suggests that parents should always support the coach "unless the coach is being inappropriately tough or critical." So I ask, where is the line between appropriate yelling and inappropriate yelling? Do athletes conditioned to be "coachable" always know? Do coaches seeking the most "coachable" athletes know? One video shared on Facebook by NCSA Athletic Recruiting under the heading "Coachable" is captioned "a great example from two professionals on how to receive coaching the right way." In the video, an NFL coach slams his headset to the ground and screams violently into two professional football players' faces. The players nod, listen, and show no visible reaction to the verbal assault. The "coachable" athlete bears the coach's outburst without question, without emotion. NCSA Athletic Recruiting finds this lack of emotional response to be a healthy reflection of "coachable" athletes. However, especially in light of my research and case study, I suggest that a training environment of fear, shame, intimidation, and inability to question authority—and the need to be "coachable"—conditions and habituates athletes over time to, by necessity, show no emotion.

What, for example, should the "coachable" athlete do when yelling turns into physical "correction?" Unfortunately, I do not need to look far for examples of coaches who have crossed this line. Indiana University head basketball coach Bobby Knight is (in)famous for throwing chairs during games. In fact, in 2015, the *Bleacher Report* celebrated the 30th anniversary of Bobby Knight throwing a chair during a game, calling it "an ejection for the ages" (Newport, 2015). A tension certainly exists in sports culture between celebrating "tough coaches" and protecting players' rights. In January 2010, University of South Florida football head coach Jim Leavitt was dismissed after he grabbed one of his players by the throat and slapped him during halftime (Milian, 2010). Leavitt was known for emotional outbursts, including head-butting players hard enough to bloody his own head. At the time of his dismissal, Leavitt was the third coach in less than six weeks to lose his job for abusive behavior. Mark Mangino had resigned as the University of Kansas head football coach after allegations of physically and psychologically abusing players, and Texas Tech fired head football coach Mike Leach after he mistreated a player who had suffered a concussion (Milian, 2010). Based on these events, Patrik Jonsson (2010) wondered if the era of the "coach-king" was over, writing that "a coach's words and actions are subject to challenge—an improvement when it uncovers abusive coaches but a possible demerit when it come [sic] to a coach's ability to keep discipline among players." Again, we see a tension in the sports world between protecting players' rights, allowing coaching that is "tough enough," and encouraging players to be fully "coachable." In fact, many players and parents came to these coaches' defenses after their removal because, as Jonsson puts it, "the firings contradict a central tenet of football: the ability of players to take a coach's guff like a man." In a sports culture where players must "tough it out," "take it like a man," and maintain the secrecy of the locker room, it seems unlikely that "coachable" players feel empowered to speak up about their concerns, including abuse.

In March 2019, Georgia Tech dismissed its head women's basketball coach, MaChelle Joseph, over concerns about a toxic coaching environment, including extreme cursing and yelling, name-calling, throwing objects, and pressuring players to play while injured (Rand, 2019). Later in 2019, University of California Riverside head women's basketball coach John Margaritis resigned amid an abuse investigation, including allegations of body-shaming, insulting players, and pressuring injured athletes to return to play (Steinbach, 2019). The removal of high-profile coaches accused of abuse may suggest a trend toward better protecting collegiate-level student-athletes, but the social and cultural ideal of the "coach-king" remains, as do the same coaching practices that are passed down to each new generation. Coaches tend to train the way they themselves were trained. Joan Ryan (2000) writes in *Little Girls in Pretty Boxes:*

> Coaches hold a revered place in the mythology of American sports. Few figures outside of politics and the military embody the American ideals of manliness and power as completely as our most famous coaches do.... These coaches' exhortations are imprinted on the national psyche, reaching beyond sports: "Winning is the only thing"; "Nice guys finish last"; "Show me a good loser and I'll show you a loser."... Hollywood has reinforced the mythic image of coaches.
>
> (p. 228)

Whether real or fictional, we are used to seeing images of coaches throwing tantrums (and sometimes objects) on the sidelines, yelling at their teams with drill sergeant zeal, humiliating underperforming players, etc. Because of long-held athletic ideals of coachability, discipline, and unquestioned authority, abusive language and behavior have too often been excused under the guise of standard sports training aimed at making players "tough enough."

I argue that speaking up for oneself is hindered over time when athletes are constantly conditioned to obey authority without question. During her testimony at Larry Nassar's January 2018 sentencing hearing in Ingham County, Michigan, gymnast Chelsea Williams specifically targeted the training culture of elite gymnastics and aspects of discipline and obedience that mirror the goals of "coachability" as creating an environment in which Nassar could abuse without question. "In the gymnastics culture I and other victims experienced, [coaches] are trusted and obeyed without question," said Williams. She stated that elite gymnastics training since childhood "results in a lifetime of obedience and engrained trust in coaches and staff that cannot be underestimated as a factor in this case of abuse." Bailey Lorencen likewise testified in Ingham County that things "weren't always by the book" in gymnastics training culture. "You do what you're told, you see who you're supposed to see, you don't talk back, and you most certainly don't ask questions about this amazing doctor that you're supposed to feel lucky to have," said Lorencen. Ryan (2000) writes:

> A gymnast on the elite level learns to stand still—mouth closed, eyes blank—and weather her coach's storms. A gymnast is seen and not heard. Even when she's in pain, she says nothing... Even when she's scared, the gymnast says nothing. *Especially* when she's scared.
>
> (pp. 35–36)

In elite programs, the "coachable" athlete often translates into the athlete who does not complain, ask questions, or show discomfort. In highly competitive programs, the consequences of speaking up—even for perfectly reasonable purposes—may mean getting cut from the program and being replaced by other more "coachable" athletes. As I will discuss later in my analysis of victim impact statements at Larry Nassar's sentencing hearings, Nassar's victims faced numerous obstacles to speaking up about their abuse, including the inability to speak about any concerns and to question authority figures. In acquiescing to Larry Nassar's "treatments," many young athletes were simply being "coachable."

Athletic values and the "sports ethic"

Top athletes hold a celebrity status worldwide, some rivaling Hollywood superstars. Whether Pelé in Brazil, Usain Bolt in Jamaica, Lionel Messi in Argentina, or LeBron James in the U.S., hero-athletes are adored by fans across the globe. Some athletes leverage sports fame into political careers, while others cross over into acting, television, endorsements, and their own businesses. *Smithsonian* magazine's list of the 100 most significant Americans of all time includes athletes like Babe Ruth, Muhammad Ali, Jackie

Robinson, Arnold Schwarzenegger, Michael Jordan, and Hulk Hogan (Frail, 2014). While, across the board, the most famous and influential athletes listed are almost exclusively men (another argument for another day), athletes like Simone Biles, Venus and Serena Williams, and Danica Patrick have capitalized on both fame and endorsement/entrepreneurial success.

I begin here by considering the connection between fame and athletics because the idea of "celebrity" played such a big (and, for me, unexpected) role in this case study. As I will outline in detail in Chapter 4, Nassar's celebrity status as a world-renowned gymnastics doctor was one of the most common reasons his victims cited for not questioning his procedures and speaking up about their experiences. Fame matters in the sports world. Even during the sentencing hearings, I noticed that prosecuting attorney Angela Povilaitis introduced the most famous gymnasts differently, including slightly longer introductions for them. Even within the context of their testimony about abuse, fame mattered. Media coverage of the trials and the subsequent movement for action against USA Gymnastics and other Nassar enablers has centered on better-known gymnasts like Aly Raisman and other Olympians. Victim 48, who made impact statements in both Eaton and Ingham Counties, stressed that it was important to hear her voice, in part, because she was just a "no name high school athlete." She stated that:

> Even though I am not a famous gymnast, I still matter, and my story is relevant.... all of the media attention on gymnasts and not what [Nassar] did has taken the focus away and may deter girls like me to come forward.

Fame is both a goal and a shared preoccupation for athletes, and once celebrity status is achieved, media and marketers are quick to capitalize on it.

The thought of athletic advertising might bring to mind images of strong, attractive athletes, glistening with sweat while performing amazing feats to plug athletic apparel, shoes, and sports drinks. As with any celebrity ethos, marketers draw on consumers' desires to be more like their hero-athletes. Fans want to look like them, dress like them, eat like them, train like them, play like them, and win like them. The way companies market to and about athletes therefore reveals social beliefs and values related to athletes; what we value is what sells. One Gatorade advertisement, for example, makes a clever use of advertising a sporting hero, Olympic gold medal sprinter Usain Bolt. The advertisement is almost entirely centered on Bolt, with his striking image on the track and the slogan "Bolt Pushes Past the Sweat" taking up most of the design's visual weight. The Gatorade bottle and branding are, by comparison, more subtle, but the message is clear: Be like Bolt. Drink Gatorade. The celebrity of the "fastest man in the world" is the central marketing strategy, reflecting athletic values like winning, being the best, training hard, and pushing past discomfort.

I find one powerful reflection of athletic values in perhaps the most iconic slogan marketed to athletes, Nike's three-word call to action: Just Do It. In 1988, Nike introduced their "Just Do It" advertising campaign with a simple ad showcasing their logo and slogan alongside a commercial featuring an 80-year-old runner named Walt Stack. One of the ad executives who developed the campaign said his team was trying to write a slogan that spoke broadly to athletes, from newcomers to world-class athletes (Bostock, 2019).

So, what does it mean for an athlete to "just do it"? The somewhat gory inspiration for the slogan is reportedly based on the final words of death row inmate Gary Gilmore, who told his firing squad: "Let's do it" (Bostock, 2019). Indeed, the slogan suggests that the road to athletic greatness, aside from using Nike products, involves a willingness to stare down one's own fear and to do literally anything. As Ivan De Luce (2013) writes, "those three words summed up the brand: do whatever it takes to win, no questions asked." The athletic values encapsulated in such a slogan are beliefs like pushing your limits, pushing through pain and discomfort, no complaints/excuses, and winning at all costs.

"Just Do It" as a marketing slogan is simple, direct, and memorable. "Just doing it" as a habituated practice in sports training, however, is much more complex, especially in studying the costs that are actually associated with winning at all costs. Lay, for example, this slogan's "just do it without complaint" value alongside the testimony of Victim 242 at Larry Nassar's Eaton County sentencing hearing. As she was being assaulted by Nassar, Victim 242 recalls thinking "if this is the only way to help me practice, then I guess I will have to suck it up and let him do it." Or consider Amanda Smith's self-rationalization when she spoke in Ingham County: "it may hurt now but he's a doctor, a God, he knows what he's doing, just suck it up." Marta Stern endured Nassar's treatments because she was "raised with the no pain, no gain mentality" from her parents and coaches.

Just doing it without complaint also reflects the expectation that athletes will push through physical pain and discomfort. When gymnast Emily Meinke fell off the bars and severely injured her back, her coach convinced her that she was fine. She testified in Ingham County that, "[my coach] told me to suck it up, to practice through the pain." That pain she was told to practice through ended up being an L-5 stress fracture. Later in her statement, Meinke elaborates on a sports culture where gymnasts are expected to push through the pain:

> In a world of club gymnastics, children are conditioned to ignore warning signs and to persevere, to dedicate their bodies and minds to do whatever it takes to achieve the highest accolades with no regard for the consequences. I am here to tell you that it's not worth it. Nothing is worth this abuse.

In Bayle Pickel's statement in Ingham County, she recounts that her coach, Twistars owner John Geddert, told her to "stop being a fucking baby" when she tore her Achilles tendon during a mount. "[Geddert] then proceeded to tell me to stop limping and continue competing no matter what the pain was.... screamed at me and threw ice at me in front of all of the coaches," said Pickel. I am not suggesting that Nike's slogan advocates for child abuse. However, I do argue that athletic marketing strategies like "Just Do It" put forth and reproduce social values and expectations for our hero-athletes like "playing through the pain" that potentially put athletes at risk. Likewise, athletes under constant pressure to "suck it up" and perform without complaints, like Pickel and Meinke, do not feel empowered to speak up about discomfort, pain, abuse, and other perfectly legitimate concerns.

Sociologists Robert Hughes and Jay Coakley (1991) coined the term "the sports ethic" to describe the norms that athletes identify with as members of a sports culture. Core ideas of the sports ethic include making sacrifices for the game, striving for distinction, accepting risks and playing through the pain, and refusing to accept limits (Hughes & Coakley, 1991). Similarly, sociologist Howard Nixon (1993) describes a "culture of risk" as the beliefs athletes are socialized into that make them more likely to accept risk, pain, and injury. Athletes accept risks, make sacrifices, and play through the pain based on various internal and external pressures. Yet over-conformity to this sports ethic can have physical and psychological consequences for athletes, such as furthering injury, avoiding or delaying medical treatment, and prioritizing winning over physical wellbeing (Jessiman-Perreault & Godley, 2016). Geneviève Jessiman-Perreault and Jenny Godley (2016) surveyed students at the University of Calgary who participate in sports to better understand whether they would choose to play while injured and who/what influenced their decision. Across all sports studied, approximately 70 percent of their sample population were willing to play while injured, and they found that the "sports ethic" was a major factor in that decision (Jessiman-Perreault & Godley, 2016). A marketing slogan like "Just Do It" capitalizes on this sports ethic and the presupposition that athletes will take risks to win. Sociologist Kevin Young (2012) writes of pain normalization in institutional settings that "such normalization processes and value systems, which make themselves known to many recreational and amateur athletes as *choices,* become systematized as *prerequisites* at the elite, and certainly the professional, level" (p. 103). As we will see in the case of Larry Nassar, compliance with both risk of injury and physical/mental abuse was the outcome of an intricate system of social, institutional, and personal pressures surrounding the sports ethic. And consistent with Young's observation above, the most elite athletes had the harshest stories to tell about athletic training culture.

The risk of injury has become normalized in sport, suggesting that a "culture of champion-building" includes an assumption of risk that puts even the youngest of participants in physical danger (Pike, 2014, p. 51). In HBO's documentary *At the Heart of Gold,* Dawn Homer, mother of former gymnast Trinea Gonczar, recalls coaches telling parents point-blank that their daughters would get injured at some point in their training. Homer recalls that the overall attitude for gymnasts was that "you are going to get hurt, and you are not going to complain" (HBO, 2019, 5:30). While injury statistics for athletes are difficult to determine, Paolo David (2005) estimates that 20 percent of child athletes are potentially at risk for various types of abuse, violence, and/or exploitation (p. 7). Elizabeth Pike (2014) cites research from the National SAFE KIDS Campaign that estimates that 3.5 million children under 14 years old receive medical treatment for sports injuries each year in the United States at a cost of around $2.5 billion (p. 52). Young (2004) writes:

> In many sports and at many levels, sport is also about learning to live with pain and hurt and, for a disconcertingly large number of athletes, injury and disablement that can last well beyond

the playing years. Of the sundry badly kept secrets from the world of sport, this is surely among the worst.

(p. xi)

A 1996 article in *The New England Journal of Medicine* specifically notes the high risk of physical injury and emotional problems for elite gymnasts, particularly because training in the sport largely involves children (Tofler et al.). Risks include "repetitive stress on the developing musculoskeletal system" that can result in permanent injury or deformity, altered growth rate that stunts full adult height, and reflex sympathetic dystrophy, as well as nutritional, endocrine, and psychiatric disorders (Tofler et al., 1996, p. 281). Other studies from the field of sociology have examined athletes' experiences with and responses to injury, confirming that athletes frequently normalize injury and other ill-health resulting from sport (e.g., Nixon, 1993; Pike, 2005; Pike & Maguire, 2003; Roderick, Waddington, & Parker, 2000; Waddington, 2000). Are we listening to athletes' stories of injury? What stories do the smiles, uniforms, fanfare, scoreboards, medals, and trophies hide? One uncomfortable truth is that Dr. Nassar had access to *so many* young gymnasts because *so many* young gymnasts were living with pain. If athletes are conditioned to normalize pain and injury, while prioritizing sport performance over their physical and emotional well-being, then it seems probable that athletes are less likely to speak up about abuse.

Let's consider for a moment one very coachable child athlete, Kerri Strug. In 1992, Strug was the youngest member of the U.S. National Team at just 14 years old. Who can forget the celebrated image of Kerri Strug vaulting with an injured ankle at the 1996 Olympics in Atlanta and being carried triumphantly to the podium by Béla Károlyi? Some critics of Simone Biles' decision to pull out of the 2020 Tokyo Olympics when she clearly was not fit for the competition were quick to point to Strug's "sacrifice" in vaulting injured and willingness to "take one for the team." This image and the insinuation that Strug's second vault was a "choice" now make me feel sick inside, especially as Strug was escorted off the floor to the waiting care of Larry Nassar. In one iconic photo, a visibly suffering Strug is being helped off the floor by one allegedly abusive coach (Márta Károlyi) to the hands of another now-convicted child abuser (Nassar).

During her testimony at Larry Nassar's January 2018 sentencing hearing in Ingham County, Michigan, gymnast Chelsea Williams refers specifically to Kerri Strug's choice to vault injured as not just a reflection of a heroic athlete, but also an illustration of the every-day, not "extraordinary" decisions that elite gymnasts are condi-tioned to make. Williams said:

> [Strug] was conditioned for over a decade to be perfect in terms of her form and power as a vaulter, but she was also trained to be obedient to the needs of her coach and her team and to bear unimaginable pain as if it were normal.

In elite gymnastics training culture, where training and competing through the pain is normal, Strug was simply doing what she had been conditioned to do without complaint since she was a child. As Strug prepared to vault again on her injured ankle, coach Béla Károlyi bellowed: "You can do it! Kerri, you can do it!"

Meanwhile, media coverage and adoring fans encourage risk-taking behavior in their hero-athletes, supporting ideologies like "playing through the pain" and "sacrificing for the team" (Pike, 2014, p. 54). Two decades before Strug's famous vault, Shun Fujimoto helped Japan win the team gymnastics gold medal at the 1976 Olympics by competing on rings with a broken kneecap, which he then dislocated when he landed. Though it meant the end of his gymnastics career, Fujimoto was celebrated as a hero. An article from *The Bleacher Report* applauds the "gutsiest play-through-pain" moments in sport, like Tiger Woods playing through the 2008 U.S. Open on a broken leg and torn ACL, praising these athletes as "superhuman" (Marie, 2013). Adoring Americans expect Kerri Strug to run and vault on an injured ankle. Spectators expect Tiger Woods to compete on a broken leg and torn ACL. Fans expect Curt Schilling to pitch in the World Series after ankle surgery, blood seeping through his sock, and Philip Rivers to play quarterback in the AFC Championship with a torn ACL and injured knee. And we celebrate these superhuman feats of courage and endurance because that is what great athletes do. They just do it.

Separation of athlete and parent/guardian

In Chapter 1, I shared my experiences of being distanced from my daughter's gymnastics training and competition. Until recently, this gymnastics club had a policy that parents of team athletes could only observe their daughters' training for one week each month, known as your "watch week." My daughter has been told that she should not try to go to or speak to her parents during practice unless she is "having a heart attack" or has other serious injuries. My son has also played on a competitive soccer team. When he was training in a local U8 Academy (for players under the age of 8), his head coach requested that all parents observe practice from behind a line at the far end of the soccer field. From behind this line, parents could more or less see what their child was doing, but they could not communicate with them or hear what the coach was saying to them. In my experience with youth competitive sports training, so far, the coaches do not really seem to want me there.

Holden et al. (2015) call the relationship between coach, parent, and athlete the "athletic triangle," which can impact a child's psychological development. Each part of this triad has expected responsibilities in a "healthy" athletic triangle. For example, coaches should provide a physically and emotionally safe environment, treat players fairly, and follow a code of ethics. Parents should provide transportation, encourage practice at home, and exhibit acceptable behavior during practice and competition. Athletes should exhibit good sportsmanship, respect, a willingness to learn, and punctuality (Holden et al., 2015). I argue that free and frequent communication is also a necessary part of a healthy athletic triangle, but communication is challenging when children must speak up for themselves, especially when parents are not involved.

Efforts to force parents out of the athletic triangle and relegate them to chauffer status only are sometimes framed as a necessary means to manage "crazy" sports parents. While the characteristics that make a parent "crazy" are not fully clear, from my own experience, it is crystal clear that you do not want the "stigma" of the "crazy gym parent" attached to you or your child. Parents hesitate to speak up or ask questions for fear of becoming the "crazy parent" to owners/coaches and the subsequent consequences to their child. In this way, the accusation of "craziness" can also be used to silence or gaslight parents.

According to a blog shared on my daughter's gym Facebook page, one characteristic of the "crazy gym parent" is alleged to be over-involvement in gym happenings, gossip, and practices (Josephson, 2015). Parental over-involvement in youth sports has been criticized on a number of very legitimate grounds in the age of "helicopter parenting" (hovering to oversee every aspect of a child's life) and "tiger parenting" (a term coined by Yale Law School professor Amy Chua and her concept of "the Chinese way" to strict parenting that includes pressuring children to excel in high-status extracurricular activities). For instance, Salla and Michel (2014) studied the relationship between anxiety and parental over-involvement among youth tennis athletes. Their study concluded that parental sport over-involvement significantly predicted anxiety symptoms among elite junior tennis players. Athletes with overly involved parents may experience feelings of pressure to excel, distress, guilt, lack of enjoyment, and burnout.

Parents can undoubtedly contribute to unhealthy training conditions for their children, such as pushing them too hard to succeed, comparing them to other athletes, undermining coaches, obsessing about scores, and withholding affection for poor achievement. Tofler et al. (1996) warn of the dangers of "achievement by proxy," which is characterized by "strong parental encouragement of a potentially dangerous endeavor for the purpose of gaining fame and financial reward" (p. 281). In *Little Girls in Pretty Boxes,* Ryan (2000) also writes about the extreme lengths that parents of elite gymnasts and figure skaters are willing to go to in forging champions and, in some cases, living their own dreams through their children. Yet Ryan also acknowledges the difficult line that parents walk in supporting their children through highly competitive training, as well as parents' own fear and silencing. "[Parents] live in fear their daughters will be expelled from the gym, so they say nothing when the coaches belittle their children or push them too hard," says Ryan (2000, p. 158). Some parents fear losing their substantial investments of time and money into training if they speak up. And especially when their child is training at the best gym in the area without a reasonable alternative, parents are forced into silence for fear their child will be asked to leave or that they will be labeled "crazy." The message is clear: trust coaches without question or go somewhere else, even if owners know that going somewhere else is not a realistic option.

It is important to note here the difference in expectations between youth recreational training (i.e., playing "just for fun"), youth competitive training (where athletes compete individually or on teams in formal competitions, often with travel involved), and elite-level competitive training (i.e., athletes who might qualify for a national or Olympic team). At the elite level, in particular, the separation of athletes from their parent(s) or guardian(s) seems to widen significantly. The nation's most elite athletic training programs tend to be boarding schools, like IMG Academy, where children and youth are sent away to live and train far from their parent(s)/guardian(s). Elite athletic training camps tend to offer very limited to no opportunities for parental participation. When parents are forced out of the athletic triangle, should they trust that the coach has their child's best interests in mind? If we were to listen to the victims' voices from the Larry Nassar sentencing hearings, the answer would be a resounding "no."

The Károlyis did not want parents involved in their children's training, either. At the Károlyi gym, "parents watched workouts from a small, sparse room separated from the gym by a thick pane of soundproof glass" (Ryan, 2000, p. 39). Parents were also not allowed to accompany their children to the national team training camps. "USAG mandates that parents aren't allowed to attend camps held at the Károlyi Ranch, a secluded location with limited cell service, which helped give Nassar the environment he needed to fulfill his sick perversion," said Victim 178 during her statement at Larry Nassar's sentencing hearing in Ingham County. "The complete detachment from the outside world on top of careless and neglectful adults made the ranch the perfect environment for abusers and molesters to thrive," echoed gymnast Mattie Larson. Victim 128 and Larson refer to conditions at Béla and Márta Károlyi's ranch in Walker County, Texas, which was the designated national team training center for women's gymnastics from 2011 to 2018. The ranch is deep within the Sam Houston National Forest, about 50 miles north of Houston, and spans more than 160,000 acres near the Piney Woods region of Texas (Smothers, 2018). Cut off from their parents and any contact with the outside world, former camp attendees referred to the ranch as a "black hole" (Smothers, 2018). Larson elaborated in her testimony:

> There is an eerie feeling as soon as you step foot onto the Károlyi Ranch. It is completely removed from all civilization. In the case of an emergency, the closest hospital is so far away you'd need to be helicoptered there. To get to the ranch you must drive up a dirt road for what seems like an eternity, and the closest civilization is a high security prison 30 miles away. On top of that, there is no cell service. It's completely isolated, and that's no mistake. That is how the Károlyis wanted it.

Larson stated that training conditions on the ranch were so horrendous that she faked a concussion and was willing to physically hurt herself to get out of going to the camp and enduring the abuse that she received there. Olympic gymnast Aly Raisman has reported extremely poor nutrition, bunks crawling with bugs, and dirty showers with no soap at the ranch—on top of the physical and mental abuse she experienced there (Jenkins, 2018). Béla Károlyi described a system of acquiring and commodifying gymnasts: "You get the child at an early age; you follow her; her life is directed towards performance[.] They are living, breathing and eating the sport—in a special environment directed to the highest quality of athletic preparation" (McPhee & Dowden, 2018, p. 128). In this "special environment," without parental supervision or consent, Larry Nassar was free to perform his "treatments" on campers at the Károlyi ranch alone and in their own bedrooms. Especially at the elite level, the intentional separation of athletes from their parent(s) or guardian(s) removes an important safeguard from their sport experience and likely contributes to unreported abuse.

Ideology and sports habits

In this chapter, I have described some of the ideologies and beliefs that underpin "rhetorical cultures of champion-building" in athletic training and the potential impact they have on athletes' willingness to speak up about abuse. Toxic sports culture, as described by many of Nassar's victims, can have a significant impact on athletes' mental health—from depression, anxiety, and suicide to eating disorders and substance abuse—as well as physical consequences from training and competing while injured or at the hands of an abusive coach. At the heart of this discussion are issues of ideologies, power differentials, and culturally habituated practices. Because ideologies influence the collective actions of the people who adhere to them, understanding the ideologies that shape athletic cultures helps us understand why athletes act in certain ways. Studying rhetoric is particularly well-suited to understanding ideology because ideology must be reinforced continuously within a group through rhetorical strategies and practices (Foss, 2018).

Gymnastics training, like many sports, is intensely repetitive. A 90-second floor exercise routine performed in competition is practiced for hundreds of hours over many months. A single new skill is practiced again and again, day after day, until it is perfected. Just as the training itself is based on repetition, training techniques become ingrained, repeated, and reproduced in sports. Once it began producing champions, the Károlyi system of longer workouts, more structured training, demeaning tactics, and total subservience for young gymnasts was replicated and reproduced—and still influences the sport today. Sports are habit-forming in many ways.

Habits are adapted behaviors—things we do so often that we don't even notice them. Mark Garrett Longaker and Jeffrey Walker (2011) distinguish a "habitus" from everyday habit as "a set of socially significant behaviors that people learn, repeat, and recognize, often without conscious awareness of their recognition and repetition" (p. 240). These behaviors often have moral and ethical overtones (Longaker & Walker, 2011). Bourdieu (1990) defines the habitus as "the system of structured, structuring dispositions... which is constituted in practice and is always oriented towards practical functions" (p. 52). Bourdieu uses the term "bodily hexis" to describe the embodiment of the habitus, a "durable way of standing, speaking, walking, and thereby of feeling and thinking" grounded in culturally habituated practices (p. 70). Teaching athletes to ignore bodily signals of pain and fatigue, for instance, could be habituated over time into physical habits or bodily hexis. The culturally habituated practices learned over time in athletic training can have more sinister consequences of discouraging or preventing athletes from speaking up about bodily discomfort, including abuse.

Michael Hartill (2014) also uses Bourdieu's theoretical notion of "illusio" or "social games" to study the sexual subjection of boys in sport. Addressing the question of why victims did not speak up about abuse, Hartill argues that the investment, the illusio, of existing within the competition, which is closely tied to their mind, body, and masculine identity, made speaking up virtually impossible. He writes:

> Boys abused in sport have been drilled, not only in the technical aspects of their sport, but also to recognize the stakes of the game in which they are invested. To speak out, or act, against the game would be to "crack the game asunder," to disregard the stakes of the game. Such is the manner in which the game has been introduced to him, the sports-boy cannot feasibly entertain such an act.
>
> (p. 87)

One way that this "social game" has been articulated into popular sports culture is in the oft-repeated catchphrases "team over me," "we over me," or "there is no 'I' in 'team'." The subjugation of self to the team further discourages expressions of individual concern or discomfort.

As I will discuss in Chapter 4, many of the athletes abused by Nassar spoke about their long-term conditioning in a high-stakes, fear-based training environment that made speaking up about their abuse impossible. I argue that habituated practices—such as being "coachable;" the ideology surrounding expectations of athletes; and cultures of sports and athletic training that, among other features, separate athletes from their parent(s) or guardian(s)—actively discourage or even prevent athletes from speaking up about abuse. The habit and ideology surrounding athletic training produce multifaceted problems of speaking, silencing, and listening.

(In)human bodies

Debra Hawhee (2009) traces rhetoric's relationship with the "arts of athletic training" to ancient Greece, arguing that rhetoric's history emerged alongside and was mutually shaped by athletics and "a network of educational practices which were articulated through and by the body" (p. 3). The discipline of rhetoric, athletic training, and making meaning of and through bodies have a very long, shared, and interconnected history. Even Aristotle cautioned in *Politics* against excessive early training in Olympic champions because it "stunts the proper development of the body" (p. 303). Bodies are framed differently, and often as other-than-human, within the context of sport and athletic training. The body is likewise separated from or subjugated to the mind in order to push oneself "to the limits" and to normalize pain, risk of injury, and abuse.

Athletic instruction is unique in that, because an athlete's "tool" is his or her body, both success and failure often involve bodily consequences. The gymnast who does not do the technique correctly must climb the rope. The football player who misses the route must do extra drills. The runner who is too slow decides to take performance-enhancing drugs. Athletic instruction might also be considered the art of sculpting champions out of "unnatural" bodies, whether that be the abnormally small gymnast or the extraordinarily tall basketball player. "Some might argue that many sports require specific, even freakish, body types for participants to excel," says Ryan (2000, p. 78). The difference is that the athletes who excel in women's gymnastics tend to actually be children, who are enduring training with all the rigor of an adult. As Ryan argues, even as children, young gymnasts must push to "clear away the human flaws and limitations," seeking unnatural weight, flexibility, resistance to pain, and control of nerves (2000, p. 206).

Celia Brackenridge (2014) argues that the talent and identification programs used to recruit elite athletes focus exclusively on talent while ignoring the human, a process that commodifies the athlete, "disembodies the human being at the centre of the enterprise—the child," and undermines the prospect of protecting children's rights in elite sport (p. 14). Philosophically, Brackenridge argues that an ethical issue in constant tension in youth sport is the existential status of the athlete—human being v. human/doing or commodity (2014, p. 16). Gretchen Kerr (2014) echoes this concern for the separation of the athlete from the body, effectively rendering the athlete as an instrument to fulfill a role. Kerr writes, "those close to the athlete (coaches, trainers, commentators) and even athletes themselves refer to the athlete's body as if it or the performance it produces exists distinct from the person (in some cases even substituting for the person)" (p. 42). This detachment, she argues, is used to justify the use of drugs and even violence and abuse for the sake of improved performance (2014, p. 42). Gymnasts and their parents have also spoken of this person-body separation. "Their body is a machine and they are a person. The two are separate," says Sandy Henrich, mother of gymnast Christy Henrich (Ryan, 2000, p. 51). Former Olympian Kelly Garrison has called gymnasts "commodities" who make a living for the sport's hierarchy (Ryan, 2000, p. 54). Former Olympic gymnast Jamie Dantzcher wrote of her training: "I couldn't feel like a person anymore if I wanted to reach my dream. I felt like a robot. This became my 'normal'" (Ryan, 2000, p. xvii). The rights of the individual participant—and even their own personhood—are overshadowed or lost in the pursuit of winning.

Of particular interest to this study, Brackenridge notes that a 2009 review of Olympic-level talent identification and development programs focused entirely on performance data. Not a single athlete's *voice* was considered or reported. Separating athletic talents from the body performing them not only undermines the protection of children's rights but can also lead to issues of mental health and self-worth for the athletes (Brackenridge, 2014). A 2006 study by Jessica Fraser-Thomas and Jean Côté identified a wide range of psychosocial detriments to youth participation in sport, including feeling excessive pressure to win, injuries, eating disorders, low self-esteem, poor moral reasoning, and violence and aggression. Brackenridge concludes that the age-related pressures for elite child athletes are under-researched; if elite talent in sport is researched, it is from a cost-benefit of investment perspective; the little research available on the danger of youth sports is typically from a psychological rather than cultural/institutional perspective; and rights-based discourse in sport is very new and has not yet impacted how elite sports are governed (2014, p. 16). Susan Bissell of UNICEF has likewise argued that "evidence of violence against children in sport is undeniable but under-researched," including physical, sexual, and psychological abuse, as well as neglect (2014, p. 21). This study seeks to attend, even in a small way, to all of these calls for further research related to the pervasiveness of violence in sport.

References

Aristotle. (1995). *Politics*. Oxford: Oxford University Press.

Bissell, S. (2014). Notes on international children's rights, implications for elite sport and the work of UNICEF. In C. H. Brackenridge, & D. Rhind (Eds.), *Elite child athlete welfare* (pp. 21–24). London: Brunel University Press.

Bostock, B. (2019, August 10). The sinister story of Nike's "just do it" slogan, which was inspired by the last words of a murderer before he was executed. *Business Insider*. Retrieved from https://www.businessinsider.com/nike-just-do-it-inspired-utah-killer-gary-gilmore-2019-7

Bourdieu, P. (1990). *The logic of practice*. Stanford, CA: Stanford University Press.

Brackenridge, C. H. (2014). Setting the challenge: The ethical and research context of children's involvement in elite sport. In C. H. Brackenridge, & D. Rhind (Eds.), *Elite child athlete welfare* (pp. 13–19). London: Brunel University Press.

David, P. (2005). *Human rights in youth sport: A critical review of children's rights in competitive sports*. New York: Routledge.

De Luce, I. (2013, September 1). 26 Nike ads that shaped the brand's history. *Business Insider*. Retrieved from https://www.businessinsider.com/25-nike-ads-that-shaped-the-brands-history-2013-8

Foss, S. (2018). *Rhetorical criticism: Exploration and practice* (5th ed.). Long Grove, IL: Waveland Press.

Frail, T. A. (2014, November 17). Meet the 100 most significant Americans of all time. *Smithsonian Magazine*. Retrieved from https://www.smithsonianmag.com/smithsonianmag/meet-100-most-significant-americans-all-time-180953341/

Fraser-Thomas, J., & Côté, J. (2006). Youth sports: Implementing findings and moving forward with research. *Athletic Insight: The Online Journal of Sport Psychology*, 8(3), 12–27.

Hartill, M. (2014). The sexual subjection of boys in sport: Towards a theoretical account. In C. H. Brackenridge, & D. Rhind (Eds.), *Elite child athlete welfare* (pp. 85–92). London: Brunel University Press.

Hawhee, D. (2009). *Bodily arts: Rhetoric and athletics in ancient Greece*. Austin, TX: University of Texas Press.

Holden, S. L., Forester, B. E., Keshock, C. M., & Pugh, S. F. (2015, June 29). How to effectively manage coach, parent, and player relationships. *The Sport Journal*. Retrieved from https://thesportjournal.org/article/how-to-effectively-manage-coach-parent-and-player-relationships/

Hughes, R., & Coakley, J. (1991). Positive deviance among athletes: The implications of overconformity to the sport ethic. *Sociology of Sport Journal,* 8, 307–325.

IMG Academy (2019, August 5). *Teaching your child to be coachable.* Retrieved from https://www.imgacademy.com/news/blog/teaching-your-child-be-coachable

Jackson, B. (2017, August 2). Six ways to be more coachable. *PGA of America.* Retrieved from https://www.pga.com/archive/six-ways-be-more-coachable

Jenkins, S. (2018, March 14). Aly Raisman: Conditions at Karolyi Ranch made athletes vulnerable to Nassar. *The Washington Post.* Retrieved from https://www.washingtonpost.com/sports/olympics/aly-raisman-conditions-at-karolyi-ranch-made-athletes-vulnerable-to-nassar/2018/03/14/6d2dae56-26eb-11e8-874b-d517e912f125_story.html

Jessiman-Perreault, G., & Godley, J. (2016). Playing through the pain: A university-based study of sports injury. *Advances in Physical Education,* 6(3), 178–194.

Jonsson, P. (2010, January 8). Jim Leavitt fired: Is the era of the coach-king over? *The Christian Science Monitor.* Retrieved from https://www.csmonitor.com/USA/Society/2010/0108/Jim-Leavitt-fired-Is-the-era-of-the-coach-king-over

Josephson, A. (2015). 9 tips to cope with drama-mama or pushy-papa. *JAG Gym Blog.* Retrieved from https://annejosephson.wordpress.com/2015/08/27/9-tips-to-cope-with-drama-mama-or-pushy-papa

Kerr, G. (2014). Physical and emotional abuse of elite child athletes: The case of forced physical exertion. In C. H. Brackenridge, & D. Rhind (Eds.), *Elite child athlete welfare* (pp. 41–50). London: Brunel University Press.

Longaker, M. G., & Walker, J. (2011). *Rhetorical analysis: A brief guide for writers.* Boston, MA: Longman.

Marie, J. (2013, June 18). The gutsiest play-through-pain moments in sports. *The Bleacher Report.* Retrieved from https://bleacherreport.com/articles/1675777-the-gutsiest-play-through-pain-moments-in-sports

McPhee, J., & Dowden, J. P. (2018). *Report of the independent investigation: The constellation of factors underlying Larry Nassar's abuse of athletes.* Boston, MA: Ropes & Gray.

Milian, J. (2010, January 8). USF's Jim Leavitt latest coach to be fired or resign over allegations of player abuse. *The Palm Beach Post.* Retrieved from https://www.palmbeachpost.com/article/20100108/SPORTS/812037645

Newport, K. (2015, February 23). We remember: 30th anniversary of Bobby Knight throwing chair during game. *The Bleacher Report.* Retrieved from https://bleacherreport.com/articles/2374441-we-remember-30th-anniversary-of-bobby-knight-throwing-chair-during-game

Nixon, H. (1993). Accepting the risks of pain and injury in sport: Mediated cultural influences on playing hurt. *Sociology of Sport Journal,* 10, 183–196.

Pike, E. (2005). "Doctors just say 'rest and take Ibuprofen:'" A critical examination of the role of non-orthodox health care in women's sport. *International Review for Sociology of Sport*, 40(2), 201–219.

Pike, E. (2014). The elite child athlete and injury risk. In C. H. Brackenridge, & D. Rhind (Eds.), *Elite child athlete welfare* (pp. 51–59). London: Brunel University Press.

Pike, E., & Maguire, J. (2003). Injury in women's sport: Classifying key elements of "risk encounters." *Sociology of Sport Journal*, 20(3), 232–251.

Rand, B. (2019, March 27). Georgia Tech coach fired over alleged "toxic" culture; coach disputes the dismissal. *ABC News*. Retrieved from https://abcnews.go.com/Sports/georgia-tech-coach-fired-alleged-toxic-culture-coach/story?id=61980171

Roderick, M., Waddington, I., & Parker, G. (2000). Playing hurt: Managing injuries in English professional football. *International Review for the Sociology of Sport*, 35, 165–180.

Ryan, J. (2000). *Little girls in pretty boxes: The making and breaking of elite gymnasts and figure skaters.* New York: Grand Central Publishing.

Salla, J., & Michel, G. (2014). Parental sport over-involvement and anxiety among youth tennis athletes. *Science & Sports*, 29, S40.

Smothers, H. (2018, February 6). Everything you need to know about Karolyi Ranch. *Cosmopolitan*. Retrieved from https://www.cosmopolitan.com/ lifestyle/a15958460/karolyi-ranch/

Steinbach, P. (2019, September). UC Riverside coach resigns amid abuse investigation. *Athletic Business*. Retrieved from https://www.athleticbusiness.com/college/uc-riverside-coach-resigns-amid-abuse-investigation.html

Tofler, I. R., Stryer, B. K., Micheli, L. J., & Herman, L. R. (1996). Physical and emotional problems of elite female gymnasts. *The New England Journal of Medicine,* 335(4), 281–283.

Ungerleider, S., & Ulich, D. (Producers), & Carr, E. L. (Director). (2019). *At the heart of gold: Inside the USA Gymnastics scandal* [Motion picture]. United States: HBO.

Waddington, I. (2000). *Sport, health and drugs: A critical sociological perspective.* London: Spon.

Young, K. (2004). *Sporting bodies, damaged selves: Sociological studies of sports-related injury.* London: Elsevier.

Young, K. (2012). *Sport, violence, and society.* London: Routledge.

3 A predator in USA Gymnastics

The numbers alone tell a horrifying story: 1 man, 500+ victims, systematic abuse over more than 20 years. Larry Nassar began working as an athletic trainer for the USA Gymnastics (USAG) national team in 1986 and served as the national medical coordinator for USAG from 1996 until 2014. He also became a team physician and assistant professor at Michigan State University (MSU) in 1997. Nassar began sexually abusing underage athletes as early as 1994 under the guise of medical treatment for sports injuries, some victims as young as 6 years old. In some cases, victims could not or would not speak up about their abuse. In other cases, victims did speak up only to be ignored. For example, Olympic gymnast Dominique Moceanu had spoken out about an abusive training culture in USAG 10 years before the Larry Nassar scandal hit the news (Pucin, 2008). No action was taken. But we had been warned even before Moceanu spoke out.

In 1995, journalist Joan Ryan first published her book *Little Girls in Pretty Boxes,* a scathing exposé of the training conditions endured by elite gymnasts and figure skaters, from injuries and eating disorders, to unrelenting pressure from (sometimes abusive) coaches and parents. Nassar had begun abusing athletes the year before the book was published, and it remains a tragically prophetic warning about athletic training cultures of abuse and silencing that were ripe for a sexual predator's exploitation. In her introduction to the book's 2018 edition, Ryan addresses the Nassar sexual abuse scandal, noting that the "alarms about abuse in elite gymnastics have sounded for years," including in her own book (p. 3). "In my research I found a culture as destructive, secretive, and indifferent to the athletes' well-being as any I had seen in my years as a sports journalist," writes Ryan (p. 3). While the first edition did prompt some initial attention and criticism of coaches, parents, and the governing organizations, Ryan laments that "the outrage didn't

DOI: 10.4324/9781003349846-3

stick" because the idea of broken and abused gymnasts "didn't square with Americans' perception of the ponytailed pixies" (p. 4). Likewise, Ryan notes that some champion gymnasts had undermined the book by dismissing it as "sour-grape exaggerations from failed gymnasts" (p. 4). The gymnastics community ultimately dismissed the book as a terrible misrepresentation from the "losers," and USAG survived the controversy unharmed. Meanwhile, Nassar continued his abuse for more than 20 years.

Table 3.1 is adapted in part from the *Lansing State Journal's* timeline of Larry Nassar's sexual assaults (according to police reports, court records, and lawsuits filed), arrest, and sentencing. Though a full timeline is not included here, a substantial portion appears to demonstrate (1) the scope of the abuse, (2) the long history of reports before any action was taken against Nassar, (3) the flood of action generated by the August 2016 *IndyStar* investigation, and (4) the wide range of people in positions of power (from parents, to coaches, to college officials) who likely knew about the abuse but did nothing to protect athletes.

The fallout continues for Nassar's many enablers. According to a *Detroit News* investigation, at least 14 MSU representatives were aware of reports of sexual abuse by Nassar from at least eight women before his arrest (Kozlowski, 2018). "Too many people in power knew about the behaviors and the complaints, and yet [Nassar] continued on the payroll and abused even more students," said Education Secretary Betsy DeVos (Dwyer, 2019). The U.S. Department of Education's $4.5 million fine is the largest to date levied under the Clery Act for these types of violations and included a number of demands for changes at the university. In comparison, a $2.4 million fine was imposed against Penn State in 2016 over its handling of the Jerry Sandusky case.

Two investigations—conducted by the federal Office of Civil Rights and the office of Federal Student Aid—found that in spite of receiving reports of sexual abuse, MSU did not properly disclose the incidents, notify campus security authorities, or issue timely warnings and that the university had also violated the terms of Title IX (Dwyer, 2019). William Strampel, the former dean of MSU's college of osteopathic medicine who oversaw Nassar, was also convicted in June 2019 for his role in the scandal. Former university president Lou Anna Simon, who resigned hours after Nassar's sentencing in federal court, faced charges of lying to law enforcement about Nassar (Mack, 2019). The charges were ultimately dismissed. MSU Gymnastics coach Kathie Klages announced her retirement

Table 3.1 Timeline of Larry Nassar's abuse and prosecution

Date	Event
1986	Nassar joins the USAG National Team medical staff as an athletic trainer.
1994	Nassar begins sexually abusing Olympic gymnast Jamie Dantzscher.
1996	Nassar is appointed National Medical Coordinator for USAG and attends his first Olympics with the team.
1997	Nassar becomes a team physician and assistant professor at MSU. The same year, a parent raises concerns to John Geddert (owner of Gedderts' Twistars USA Gymnastics Club in Dimondale, Michigan) about Nassar, but Geddert doesn't notify police.
1997	Larissa Boyce reports Nassar's abuse to MSU Gymnastics coach Kathie Klages, but allegedly Klages discourages Boyce from filing a complaint.
1998	Nassar begins sexually abusing the 6-year-old daughter of a family friend. That same year, a student-athlete at MSU reports concerns about Nassar to trainers or coaches, but the university takes no action.
2000	A second student-athlete at MSU reports concerns regarding Nassar to trainers or coaches, and the university again takes no action.
2004	The alleged victim in Nassar's Ingham County charges tells her parents about the sexual abuse but they do not report it to police.
2014	MSU clears Nassar of any wrongdoing just months after a graduate complains he sexually assaulted her during a medical examination.
2014	Rachael Denhollander reports her abuse to a fellow coach to dissuade other athletes from going to Nassar for treatment. Her abuse began in 2000 when she was 15.
June 17, 2015	Maggie Nichols' coach, Sarah Jantzi, learns of Nassar's sexual abuse of Nichols and two other gymnasts and notifies USAG executives. USAG president Steve Penny does not immediately notify police.
Aug. 4, 2016	The *IndyStar* publishes its investigation into USAG: "A blind eye to sex abuse: How USA Gymnastics failed to report cases."
Aug. 29, 2016	Rachael Denhollander files a criminal complaint against Nassar with MSU Police.

(Continued)

Date	Event
Aug. 30, 2016	MSU relieves Nassar of clinical and patient duties.
Sept. 8, 2016	Jamie Dantzscher files a civil lawsuit in California alleging sexual abuse by Nassar from 1994 to 2000.
Sept. 12, 2016	Denhollander and Dantzscher publicly accuse Nassar of sexual abuse in an *IndyStar* report: "Former USA Gymnastics doctor accused of abuse."
Sept. 20, 2016	MSU fires Nassar from his position as an associate professor in the College of Osteopathic Medicine.
Nov. 22, 2016	Nassar is charged in Ingham County with three counts of first-degree criminal sexual conduct with a person under 13. Officials report around 50 complaints received from victims alleging sexual abuse.
Dec. 16, 2016	Nassar is indicted on federal child pornography charges for receiving or attempting to receive images of child pornography in 2004 and for possessing child pornography between 2003 and 2016.
Dec. 21, 2016	Nassar is denied bond on the federal charges. Investigators found at least 37,000 images and videos of child pornography on Nassar's personal hard drives.
Jan. 10, 2017	Eighteen victims file a federal lawsuit against Nassar, MSU, USAG, and John Geddert's Twistars USA Gymnastics Club, alleging sexual assault, battery, molestation, and harassment between 1996 and 2016.
	The lawsuit alleges that victims raised concerns to MSU coaches or trainers in both 1999 and 2000, but the university failed to investigate. The lawsuit also alleges that in 1997 a parent raised concerns to Geddert, who didn't report them to police.
	According to the lawsuit, allegations were also made to the Meridian Township Police Department in 2004.
Feb. 13, 2017	MSU Gymnastics coach Kathie Klages is suspended by the university after Larissa Boyce claims in court records that Klages had discouraged her from filing a sexual assault complaint against Nassar in 1997.
Feb. 14, 2017	Kathie Klages announces her retirement. A second gymnast alleges that Klages discouraged her from reporting Nassar's conduct.
Feb. 22, 2017	Police secure warrants for 22 new sexual assault charges against Nassar related to his work at MSU and Twistars USA Gymnastics Club.

June 30, 2017	Twenty-three women and girls join a federal lawsuit against Nassar, MSU, and USAG, bringing the total number of claimants to 119.
Oct. 18, 2017	McKayla Maroney publicly states that she was abused by Nassar in a Twitter post. Weeks later, Aly Raisman said during a *60 Minutes* interview that Nassar abused her. And in a November Instagram post, Gabby Douglas said Nassar sexually assaulted her.
Nov. 22, 2017	Nassar pleads guilty to seven counts of first-degree criminal sexual conduct in Ingham County Circuit Court as part of a plea agreement.
Nov. 29, 2017	Nassar pleads guilty to three counts of first-degree criminal sexual conduct in Eaton County Circuit Court as part of a plea agreement.
Dec. 7, 2017	Nassar is sentenced to 60 years in federal prison on child pornography charges.
Dec. 20, 2017	Olympic gymnast McKayla Maroney files a lawsuit against the U.S. Olympic Committee, USAG, and MSU for the organizations' failures to "properly investigate, discipline, or remove" Nassar after complaints of sexual abuse.
Jan. 22, 2018	John Geddert is suspended from USAG. Hours after the suspension announcement, Geddert says in letter to families that he is retiring.
Jan. 24, 2018	Judge Rosemarie Aquilina sentences Nassar to 40 to 175 years in prison on sexual assault charges in Ingham County. In total, 156 women and girls made statements over the 7-day hearing. MSU President Lou Anna Simon resigns hours after Nassar was sentenced amid calls for her resignation.
Feb. 5, 2018	Judge Janice Cunningham sentences Nassar to 40–125 years in prison in Eaton County, bringing an end to his criminal cases.
May 16, 2018	MSU agrees to a $500 million settlement with the hundreds of women and girls who say Nassar sexually assaulted them.
Sept. 5, 2019	The U.S. Department of Education levies a $4.5 million fine against MSU for failing to address Nassar's sexual abuse of athletes.
Feb. 25, 2021	John Geddert is charged with human trafficking, sexual assault, racketeering, and lying to a police officer. Hours later, he dies by suicide.
Dec. 13, 2021	USAG and the U.S. Olympic Committee agree to a $380 million settlement with Nassar's victims, ending a 5-year legal battle.

immediately after two gymnasts alleged that she discouraged them from reporting Nassar's abuse. In February 2020, she was found guilty on charges of lying to police, though the Michigan Court of Appeals later vacated the conviction (Kozlowski, 2021). During the trial, Larissa Boyce testified that after telling Klages of Nassar's abuse in 1997, Klages held up a piece of paper and said, "Well, I could file something but there's going to be serious consequences both for you and Dr. Nassar. I was *silenced.* I wasn't going to say anything else" (Barr & Murphy, 2020 [emphasis added]).

Though Larry Nassar is now behind bars, the impacts of the scandal on the USAG organization are still unfolding. USAG and the U.S. Olympic and Paralympic Committee (USOPC) have faced dozens of lawsuits from victims. In January 2018, after Nassar's sentencing, the entire board of USAG resigned to comply with a USOPC demand. The following month, USAG CEO Scott Blackmun resigned for "health reasons." In November 2018, the USOPC filed a complaint initiating a Section 8 proceeding against USAG to strip the organization of its national governing body status. With most of its sponsors gone, USAG filed for bankruptcy protection in early December 2018. Though Kathryn Carson, the new chair of the USAG board, claimed the move was primarily to expedite victim claims, victims' attorney John Manly called the bankruptcy filing "the inevitable result of the inability of this organization to meet its core responsibility of protecting its athlete members from abuse" (Axon et al., 2018). USAG had still not learned the lesson of listening to its own athletes when replacing Blackmun as CEO. The organization revolved through three new CEOs in two years and faced criticism from a number of athletes for ignoring their concerns when choosing new leadership. The future of the USAG organization remains uncertain.

The history and culture of abuse toward young gymnasts in USAG likely extend beyond the specific actions of Nassar and, in fact, may have created an ideal environment for a sexual predator to perpetuate his crimes without consequences. Even as I conducted this research, the case continued to unfold in unsettling ways. In February 2020, USAG proposed a $215 million settlement with 517 of Nassar's victims that, if accepted, would release key players and potential Nassar enablers from further investigation and liability, including Steve Penny, the former president and CEO of USAG; the USOPC; and Béla and Márta Károlyi (Catherman & Lear, 2020). Olympic gymnast Aly Raisman immediately criticized the move, tweeting:

> The problem is USAG & USOC don't want anyone to know. This is a massive cover up. The only way for anyone to know

what really happened is if someone forces them to release ALL documents & data to investigate. HOW CAN WE MAKE THIS HAPPEN?

Catherman and Lear (2020)

Olympian Simone Biles echoed Raisman's frustration and has repeatedly called for accountability and an independent investigation of Nassar (Catherman & Lear, 2020). To Raisman and Biles, the *institutional* response to Nassar's victims thus far has been one of silencing and self-preservation rather than listening to victims' concerns.

Studying a wicked problem

In the introduction to this book, I have suggested that the problem of abuse in youth and college athletics is a *wicked problem* that cannot be solved by one person or one study. Returning to a wicked problems approach, I would emphasize up front that my focus is on one sport/case of a much larger issue that has, thus far, been under-researched in any field. The problem of protecting young athletes is much broader than a single sport and one abusive doctor, and like all truly wicked problems, it defies any simple solution. Its study cannot be assigned to a single discipline, nor should it be approached from any singular angle. For my part, I aimed to do what rhetoricians ought to do well—listen. I listened to the words of the survivors, to the messages they received during their training, and to the stories they were silenced from telling. Rather than apply a specific, predetermined theoretical lens to these stories, I sought instead to listen, analyze, and understand how athletes' testimonies can shape and inform our understanding of athletic training cultures.

This project centers on the following research questions to explore the relationship between organization, violence, and silence in youth and college sports programs:

1 Are systems and rhetorics of *silencing* embedded in youth and intercollegiate athletics organizations, and, if so, what impact do they have on athletes?
2 How do the rhetoric and discursive practices of youth and college athletic programs impact athletes' willingness to speak up about abuse?

This book presents an analysis of silence and silencing in sports programs using a case study of the Larry Nassar scandal at MSU and within USAG. It foregrounds the victims' voices through an analysis of victim impact statements and victim interviews, while examining other textual artifacts to understand the institutional behaviors and actions both before and after the case caught public attention. I interrogate the habits, ideologies, and training techniques that contributed to a culture of abuse at MSU and within USAG, with a specific focus on silence and silencing in athletic "rhetorical cultures of champion-building."

Case study research

According to Sonja Foss (2018), ideological criticism should culminate in discovering how the ideology revealed from the texts analyzed functions for the audience and the consequences it has in the world (p. 248). Case study is a form of naturalistic inquiry, or study of human behavior in its natural or customary contexts, that involves a detailed examination of a single subject, group, or phenomenon (Frey et al., 2000). Jean Hartley argues that case study is not actually a method but a research strategy in which "the context is deliberately part of the design" (2004, pp. 323–324). A case study can include multiple methods, both qualitative and quantitative, but is better defined in terms of its theoretical focus to give the details studied wider significance (Hartley, 2004). Hartley writes:

> The key feature of the case study approach is not method or data but the emphasis on understanding processes as they occur in their context. Research questions about "how" and "why" rather than "what" or "how much" are best suited to the case study strategy. The emphasis is not on divorcing context from the topic under investigation but rather to see this as a strength and to explore the interactions of phenomena and context.
>
> (p. 332)

In organizational research, case studies center around groups and individuals operating within or around one or more organizations (Hartley, 2004). A case study of the Larry Nassar scandal at MSU and within USAG helps us understand the impact of sports rhetoric and ideology on athletes. This particular case study is aimed at better understanding the institutional/organizational values, ideologies, and processes *over time* that led to the silencing of athletes.

The timeline outlined in Table 3.1 begins in 1994 when the first known case of Nassar's abuse began, but we will focus specifically on the time from publication of the August 2016 *IndyStar* report and subsequent investigation into USAG and MSU to the sentencing of Larry Nassar. Because this study examines a single group of individuals over time in the context of their athletic training and competition within specific institutions, and because it seeks to answer both the *how* and *why* of rhetorics of silencing, the case study approach is appropriate.

This study also includes elements of institutional ethnography and institutional critique, particularly in analyzing the response of USAG and MSU to the Larry Nassar case. Porter et al. (2000) call for institutional critique as an "activist methodology for changing institutions" and countering oppressive institutional structures (p. 610). They argue that "since institutions are rhetorical entities, rhetoric can be deployed to change them" (p. 610). Institutional critique can therefore be used as a methodology that bridges both theory and practice.

Institutional critique helps us understand why and how organizations/institutions operate and how individuals and groups interact with them and within them. Michelle LaFrance and Melissa Nicolas (2012) define institutional ethnography as a methodology for "explicating, and thereby gaining insight into, the actualities" of institutions (p. 131). According to LaFrance and Nicolas, the goal of institutional ethnography research is to "uncover *how things happen*—what practices constitute the institution as we think of it, how discourse may be understood to compel and shape those practices, and how norms of practice speak to, for, and over individuals" (p. 131). Institutional ethnography must therefore be centered within the discourses of the institution. Here, we examine the rhetorical practices of institutions like USAG and how those discourses have shaped individual athletes' experiences. It is typical for case studies to employ multiple methods, again because case studies are better articulated as a research strategy rather than a method. In fact, Yin (1994) suggests that the use of multiple methods is part of the definition of case study research. This case study therefore employs methods of institutional ethnography, content analysis, narrative inquiry, and ideological analysis (described below).

Two studies of sports institutions align closely with this study topic—Kristy McCray's article on intercollegiate athletes and sexual violence and Kate Lockwood Harris's book on Title IX and sexual violence on U.S. campuses. While neither McCray nor Harris hail from English departments, both draw from feminist and feminist new materialist theory. Primarily studying acts of violence against women by male student-athletes, sport management professor McCray (2015) calls for more quantitative and qualitative study of the context and environments where student-athlete violence against women occurs (p. 442). Specifically, she calls for a more interdisciplinary approach and a different theoretical framework—new and feminist institutionalism—for researching college sports programs as institutions with norms, values, and expected behaviors.

Harris (2019), a communication professor, asks, "How are organization and violence related, and what does that relationship have to do with communication?" (p. 1). She investigates the problem of Title IX and sexual assault on college campuses and how organizations respond to sexual violence. Drawing from feminist new materialism and communication theory, Harris considers "how complex physical and symbolic components of violence are embedded in organizations" (p. 1). She "looks beyond" moments of physical injury, which are often the sole focus of "violence," to other forms of organizational violence and the complex systems that influence what happens on college campuses to understand sexual violence as a "continuously organized, material-discursive phenomenon" (p. 3). In connection to Title IX, I ask a related question: How are organization and silence related? What systems and rhetorics of silencing are embedded in intercollegiate athletics organizations, and what impact does that have on student-athletes?

In terms of generalizing from cases studies, Hartley (2004) argues that case studies should focus on analytical generalization because their primary goal is usually building theory and generating hypotheses rather than testing them. Hartley writes:

> The detailed examination of processes in context can reveal processes which can be proposed as general or as specific to that organization. The detailed knowledge of the organization and especially the knowledge about the *processes* underlying the behaviour and its *context* can help to specify the conditions under which the behaviour can be expected to occur. In other words, the generalization is about theoretical propositions not about populations.
>
> (p. 331)

I recognize that generalizing the phenomena described in this study beyond the specific case and sports studied is potentially problematic. However, I may theorize that the processes and discourses that led to silencing behaviors in the context of athletes' experiences within USAG and at MSU may be applicable to other organizations and sports, especially if they share the same ideologies, beliefs, behaviors, training techniques, and discourse practices. Again, further critical study and empirical research on the experiences of athletes in other youth and college-level sports programs is warranted, particularly as they relate to violence and silence.

Analysis of silence and silencing in USAG and MSU

Larry Nassar's prison sentences may arguably have been a form of "justice" for his victims, but the consequences, healing, and greater impact on the sport of gymnastics did not end with the court proceedings. As we now know, both MSU and USAG had received complaints about Nassar years before the case caught public attention but took no significant action. The owners of Gedderts' Twistars USA Gymnastics Club—where Larry Nassar volunteered on Monday nights—had also received multiple complaints about Nassar's treatments but acted only to protect the doctor while shaming victims. The fallout from the scandal is still unfolding, including hundreds of lawsuits and recent threats by the USOPC to disband USAG as the sport's governing body.

For the case study, I analyzed the following artifacts:

1 January and February 2018 victim impact statements during the sentencing of Larry Nassar in Ingham County and Eaton County, Michigan.
2 Ungerleider, S., & Ulich, D. (Producers), & Carr, E. L. (Director). (2019). *At the heart of gold: Inside the USA Gymnastics scandal* [Motion picture]. United States: HBO.
3 "USA Gymnastics," a *60 Minutes* episode that aired on February 19, 2017. It includes interviews with former gymnasts Jamie Dantzscher, Jessica Howard, and Jeanette Antolin (CBS News, 2017).
4 The original *IndyStar* report on sex abuse in USAG: https://www.indystar.com/story/news/investigations/2016/08/04/usa-gymnastics-sex-abuse-protected-coaches/85829732/
5 "The Courage of Survivors: A Call to Action," released on July 30, 2019. This is a Congressional report investigating the actions of the USOPC and USAG in response to the Nassar case (U.S. Senate, 2019).

6 The Michigan House of Representatives' official inquiry concerning MSU's handling of the Larry Nassar investigation, released on April 5, 2018 (Kesto et al., 2018).

I chose the first three artifacts as the best publicly available, first-hand accounts of the athletes' experiences within their training programs and with Larry Nassar. I recognize that one of the limitations of these texts is that they could be considered "public performance," either during legal hearings or for media productions. Especially in a study of silence and silencing, I must acknowledge that speaking publicly and speaking privately may generate different responses. And, as Peter Smagorinsky (2008) warns, interviews "are not benign but rather involve interaction effects" such as interviewer behavior and body language (p. 395). I must, as Cheryl Glenn (2004) does in *Unspoken* in her analysis of Anita Hill, listen to these interviews and this testimony rhetorically.

I chose to include the original *IndyStar* report, Congressional report, and Michigan House of Representatives inquiry as evidence of the action/inaction taken by various organizations to protect young gymnasts. I examined these texts to understand the institutional behaviors and actions both before and after the case caught public attention. While these three texts are not part of the qualitative content analysis described below, they offer insights into the overall context, which is crucial to case study research.

Qualitative content/theme analysis

For this case study, I conducted content/theme analysis of texts 1–3 identified in the previous section. In particular, I analyzed these artifacts for references related to silencing, such as unwillingness, inability, or fear of speaking up. This study examined USAG and MSU athletes' testimony and interviews collectively to identify common themes, patterns, and shared experiences. I call this part of the study "qualitative content analysis" based on Frey et al.'s (2000) description of this method, whereby researchers are interested in determining the meanings and themes associated with messages (in contrast to quantitative analysis, when researchers count the number of times message variables occur). In qualitative content analysis, researchers analyze discourse to understand how language is used in specific social, cultural, and organizational contexts to reinforce and reproduce shared beliefs and practices. Penny

Dick (2004) writes that "discourses effectively produce different versions of what counts as 'normal' social practice" in different domains (p. 204). We therefore look to the discourse of individuals, groups, and organizations to understand its impact on the way members speak and act—in this case their willingness to speak up about abuse.

Theme analysis, in particular, describes my approach to identifying reoccurring themes in the interviews and victim impact statements related to Larry Nassar's trials. "Theme analysis is a respected and well-established and widely-used method of qualitative analysis," writes David Boje (2001, p. 112). Using Boje's descriptions of these techniques, I argue that the theme analysis I conducted in this research employs both deductive analysis (identifying, categorizing, and coding themes) and antenarrative theme analysis (looking between and beyond narrative themes) approaches. I used deductive analysis methods to search transcripts of interviews and victim impact statements to identify repeated narrative themes. I mapped these themes to understand commonalities, patterns, and shared descriptions that help explain victims' experiences. However, I also suggest that this study included aspects of antenarrative theme analysis. Boje explains that "an antenarrative approach to theme analysis is about what gets left out of the themes and taxonomy cages and what goes on between cells. What is beyond the map?" (2001, p. 114). Because my goal was also to interrogate the institutions at the heart of the Larry Nassar scandal, I was also concerned with how all of these stories connect within a specific time, place, and culture. I sought to answer both the *how* and *why* of rhetorics of silencing. I listened, for example, to what victims told us *outside* of the expected function of a victim impact statement. I listened to what the victims said about how they were talked to, how they were trained, and why they did not feel they could speak up about abuse. In the next section, I discuss victim impact statements as sites of narrative inquiry, their functions and purposes within the U.S. criminal justice system, and their expected themes.

Victim impact statements as sites of narrative inquiry

During his trial in Ingham County, Larry Nassar pleaded guilty to seven counts of first-degree criminal sexual conduct with minors under the age of 16 that occurred in Ingham County. During the Eaton County trial, Nassar pleaded guilty to three counts of criminal sexual conduct that occurred at Gedderts' Twistars USA

Gymnastics Club between September 2009 and September 2011. As part of the plea agreement in both trials, Judge Rosemarie Aquilina (Ingham County) and Judge Janice K. Cunningham (Eaton County) allowed all survivors who wished to present victim impact statements to the Court during the sentencing hearings. In all, between the two hearings, 204 survivors presented statements—some in person; some via video; and some read by court officials, parents, or other relations.

According to the U.S. Department of Justice, victims exercise their right to be reasonably heard at sentencing through victim impact statements, which can be either written or oral statements. The United States Attorney's Office, District of Alaska, lists several purposes of a victim impact statement. A victim impact statement helps the Court understand how the crime has impacted the victim emotionally, physically, and financially and helps the judge decide both an appropriate sentence and (if applicable) orders for the defendant to pay restitution ("Victim Impact Statements," 2020). The U.S. Attorney's Office suggests that a victim impact statement also "provides an opportunity to express in your own words what you, your family, and others close to you have experienced as a result of the crime" and notes that "many victims also find it helps provide some measure of closure to the ordeal the crime has caused" ("Victim Impact Statements," 2020). Therefore, victim impact statements are written, at least in part, to fulfill these specific purposes within the criminal justice system and the performance of a trial. Based on these purposes, some expected themes for the victim impact statements in Larry Nassar's trials included physical, emotional, and financial impacts of Nassar's abuse; negative impacts to the victims' families and relationships; and expressions of closure. While these themes are certainly present, as described in Chapter 4, the statements also covered a wide variety of additional themes and apparent purposes.

It is important to note here also that victim impact statements are specific types of discourse with unique rhetorical considerations. They are a form of public rhetoric, often with purposes beyond the courtroom. Amy Propen and Mary Lay Schuster (2010) see a victim impact statement as a tool for advocacy that "functions as a mediating device through which advocates push for collective change, particularly for judicial acceptance of personal and emotional appeals" (p. 3). Two recent studies have interrogated the purpose and rhetorical potential of victim impact statements, specifically focusing on the Nassar hearings. Katie Gibson (2021) argues that the "collective rhetoric" of so many survivors sharing their stories at the Nassar hearings served to "disrupt courtroom norms, hegemonic scripts, and generic expectations that contain and diminish testimony of sexual violence" (p. 519). Therefore, victim impact statements can have a subversive potential, especially when fueled by "collective anger," though Gibson argues that this potential is limited by race, power, and privilege (2021, p. 519). Shari Stenberg (2022) specifically focuses on concepts of betrayal in the impact statements, both Nassar's betrayal and the institutional betrayal of the organizations and authorities involved. Stenberg calls this "unacknowledged betrayal" and suggests that the collective act of sharing victim impact statements allowed survivors "to shift the shame and responsibility they have internalized to call for the need to acknowledge the cultural problem of unacknowledged betrayal in order to prevent sexual predation and to support survivors" (2022, p. 49).

I consider the victim interviews and impact statements studied here as a form of organizational storytelling. Yiannis Gabriel and Dorothy Griffiths (2004) suggest that "stories also open valuable windows into the emotional and symbolic lives of organizations, offering researchers a powerful research instrument" (p. 114). I do not mean storytelling here in the sense of organizational lore, as you might find in a business reproducing the almost mythical stories of its founders and/or hero-leaders. Rather, I suggest that victims telling their stories is an important focus of research that seeks to understand the policies, practices, collective ideologies, and values that shaped victims' shared experiences. Connelly and Clandinin (2006) call this study of storytelling "narrative inquiry." They write:

> Narrative inquiry, the study of experience as story... is first and foremost a way of thinking about experience. Narrative inquiry as a methodology entails a view of the phenomenon. To use narrative inquiry methodology is to adopt a particular narrative view of experience as phenomena under study.
>
> (p. 477)

Narrative inquiry as a research methodology focuses on understanding our daily lives and experiences through stories grounded in place, time, and social contexts (Clandinin et al., 2007). Storytelling (in this case, through interviews and victim impact statements) is therefore a rich source for interrogating the characteristics and cultures of specific organizations and institutions. In the case of Larry Nassar, victims' stories offer significant insight into the training conditions and institutional cultures that not only failed to protect athletes but also made them unwilling or unable to speak up about their abuse.

Participants

All participants researched were women; members of USAG, artistic sports programs, and/or MSU's athletic programs; and victims of sexual abuse by Larry Nassar. I chose to exclude a small number of the victim impact statements from the study texts for various reasons. First, some of Nassar's victims who spoke at the trial were not connected to either institution (USAG or MSU), and if this was evident in their testimony, I excluded it. For example, Nassar's first reported victim, Kyle Stephens, was a family friend. However, I did choose to include a small number of victims who were athletes at MSU but not in the gymnastics program, because I still considered them as institutional participants. I also chose to broaden my focus to include not only gymnastics but other "artistic sports," specifically dance, figure skating, and cheerleading. Only 16 total victims were involved in these sports and not gymnastics. (Some participated in one of these sports but also in gymnastics.) While that is a relatively small percentage of the overall number of victims studied, I was aware that including these sports could potentially impact the study findings. In making this decision, I ultimately listened to the victims. Most memorably, Annie Labrie, a gymnast, likened figure skating and dance to gymnastics as sports that function within a "very specific culture," one that exhibits intense focus on young girls' bodies and expects purity and innocence while simultaneously oversexualizing very young athletes. Citing experiences like "crude comments, inappropriate remarks on our bodies, incredibly uncomfortable situations, consistently creepy men towering over us, and the pressure of narrow Euro-centric beauty standards," Labrie concludes that "our bodies did not belong to us." Because training in "artistic sports" (used here to describe gymnastics, figure skating, dance, and cheerleading) uniquely exhibits this shared culture and expectations surrounding girls' bodies, I chose to include participants in all of these four sports. In all, 141 of the 181 victims included in this analysis were known to have participated in gymnastics. (Some victims' sports were unavailable for reporting.)

Second, I chose to exclude statements made by parents, family members, coaches, spouses, etc. that were not from the perspective of the victim. In other words, if a parent, family member, or court official read a statement written by the victim, I included it. If the statement was written/made by or from the perspective of someone else, I excluded it. While I do consider family members to be participants in an athlete's overall experience, and in particular find value in listening to parents' voices in these cases, I chose to limit this study's focus to the participants who were actually part of the institutions studied.

Third, I excluded one statement submitted via an audio recording by an anonymous victim in Ingham County, as this statement was not recorded in the court transcript and was also cut from the live feed. And finally, since 12 victims spoke at both the Ingham and Eaton County hearings, I needed to avoid duplication in my final analysis. For each of these instances, if the statement was not excluded, I reviewed the testimony at both hearings. If they were essentially identical (i.e., tagged the same exact themes), I only included one statement in the final analysis. If they were different, I merged the statements/themes in my analysis, so that each victim "voice" only appeared once. I also combined the two statements from Jane B42 Doe and Victim 138, since they are from the same victim. Therefore, in total, my participant criteria reduced the number of victim impact statements analyzed from 218 to 192 and (because of the overlap) the total number of victim voices studied to 181.

Method of analysis

In all, my analysis of the victim impact statements alone included more than 600 pages of text. To help get a closer understanding of this large amount of textual material, my first task was to read through the testimony and interviews and note reoccurring themes. According to Frey et al. (2000), researchers use narrative approaches in qualitative content analysis to focus on major themes and stories contained in texts (p. 237). In this first reading, while I was particularly interested in references to silence, I did not limit my notations to only these references. I noted and listed all themes that reoccurred frequently throughout the texts. These themes are provided in Table 4.1. On a second reading, I made note of each instance and coded each occurrence by theme. Figure 3.1 provides an example of three excerpts from the victim impact statements and how I coded the text by theme. In all, I identified 100 repeated themes, which I then grouped into five main narrative categories: (1) ethos of Larry Nassar at the time of abuse, (2) reasons for speaking/not speaking

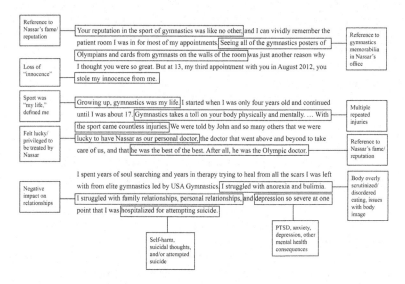

Figure 3.1 Example theme analysis of victim impact statements.

about abuse, (3) reasons for speaking at the sentencing hearing, (4) consequences of abuse, and (5) institutional culture.

Although 100 themes are a considerable amount for qualitative research (though perhaps not considering the amount of text I studied), I ultimately chose not to limit my overall analysis to just a few themes. Frankly, I was curious to listen and to hear the victims' voices comprehensively. To answer my specific research questions, however, I did capture all instances that referenced silence, including fear of speaking up, reluctance to report abuse, feelings of shame, ignoring victim reports, and intentional silencing. The final selection of interviews and testimony that are described in my analysis section is organized around each major narrative category and was meticulously gathered from the texts studied.

Victims/survivors

I recognize that language matters in this (and all) research and that the terms "victim" and "survivor" have different connotations in the context of crime. During Nassar's sentencing hearings, prosecuting attorney Angela Povilaitis was careful to use the term "survivor," even correcting herself if she accidentally referred to a speaker as a "victim." The Rape, Abuse & Incest National Network (RAINN) notes that both terms are applicable in describing people and their experiences, but tends to use the term "victim" when referring to someone who has recently been affected by sexual violence or discussing a particular crime, while "survivor" refers to someone who has gone through the recovery process or the short- or long-term effects of sexual violence ("Key Terms and Phrases").

When writing about the Nassar cases, Doyle (2019) privileges the term "victim" because her focus is "not on the recovery and survival experiences of the people he harmed, but on the scene of their disenfranchisement as subjects with the capacity to understand, know, and represent what was happening to their own bodies" (pp. 11–12). I also primarily use the term "victim" throughout this book, as I focused on the scene and circumstances of silencing, though I use the term "survivor" when writing specifically about impact statements where the speaker has referred to herself as a "survivor." In other words, in instances when the speaker's preference is known, I defer to that person's self-identified terminology. And as I indicated in my discussion of victim impact statements, one typical purpose of offering a victim impact statement is seeking personal recovery and/or closure.

Risks and limitations

One risk in this type of study is that I could only choose a finite number of texts to analyze, and therefore I may have excluded other meaningful voices from this issue. For example, Netflix's *Athlete A*—a documentary that follows the reporters, gymnasts, and legal team behind Nassar's prosecution—was released after this study was completed. I could not address all relevant texts, so I was limited to studying a sample. Because my case study is limited to the Larry Nassar scandal at MSU and within USAG, its findings may not be generalizable to other institutions and sports. This study cannot and should not be the last word.

It is also important to note that I was not a neutral participant in this study. This topic came to me as a "felt issue," as a mother whose experiences had raised concerns about her children's participation in athletic programs. While every researcher brings biases to every study, ethically, it is important for me to articulate and be transparent about my background and motivations. I also see my position as a community member within this broader study population and my investment in protecting athletes as a positive driving factor of my research.

While I did not work directly with participants in this study, it is also important to acknowledge that there is a risk of exploitation, misrepresentation, and further trauma. As Frey et al. (2000) note, by their nature, communication research projects cannot be conducted without somehow impacting the people being studied. And studying and writing about actual cases of sexual assault is challenging in many ways. While traits like impartiality and being dispassionate are valued in researchers, I feel it is important to acknowledge that conducting this type of research *is* an emotion-filled endeavor. I have not studied texts before that made me weep, but stoicism in the face of these victims' stories would not seem to be a humane response, either. Kendall Gerdes (2019) defends a more "sensitive" rhetoric, arguing that "the sensitivity of students (as well as teachers) is what actually makes teaching and learning possible" (p. 5). Gerdes writes that "sensitivity, like rhetoricity, is [an] incapacity or inability to stop oneself from being affected in language" (p. 15). Although language and representation can be traumatic and make one vulnerable, rather than viewing sensitivity as a drawback, Gerdes argues instead that sensitivity offers the opportunity for rhetorical affection and action (p. 18). Extending this argument to the role of the researcher, perhaps sensitivity to rhetorical trauma gives the researcher even more of an obligation to respond ethically and to learn from painful or difficult texts (Gerdes, 2019).

I also acknowledge a weighty ethical responsibility in interpreting and representing other peoples' stories, as well as pursuing a topic that involves significant trauma to victims. As Doyle (2019) writes, "engaging unresolved or poorly resolved cases risks contributing to the harassment dynamics internal to the case's impacted communities" (pp. 3–4). Because this was and is a highly publicized and well-documented case, Nassar's victims have already faced considerable public scrutiny. I do not wish to contribute further to their harassment or harm.

References

Axon, R., Armour, N., & Evans, T. (2018, December 5). USA Gymnastics files for bankruptcy, a move related to Larry Nassar's sexual abuse lawsuits. *USA Today*. Retrieved from https://www.usatoday.com/story/sports/olympics/2018/12/05/usa-gymnastics-files-bankruptcy-nassar-lawsuits/2218546002/

Barr, J., & Murphy, D. (2020, February 14). Former Michigan State gymnastics coach Kathie Klages found guilty of lying to police. *ESPN.* Retrieved from https://www.espn.com/college-sports/story/_/id/28703239/former-michigan-state-gymnastics-coach-kathie-klages-found-guilty-lying-police

Boje, D. (2001). *Narrative methods for organizational & communication research.* Thousand Oaks, CA: Sage.

Catherman, C., & Lear, J. (2020, March 2). Simone Biles, Aly Raisman criticize USA Gymnastics' proposed settlement for survivors of Larry Nassar's abuse. *CNN.* Retrieved from https://www.cnn.com/2020/03/02/us/simone-biles-criticizes-usa-gymnastics-sex-assault-trnd/

CBS News (2017, February 19). *60 Minutes: USA Gymnastics* [Video file]. Retrieved from https://www.cbsnews.com/video/usa-gymnastics/

Clandinin, D. J., Pushor, D., & Orr, A. M. (2007). Navigating sites for narrative inquiry. *Journal of Teacher Education,* 58(1), 21–35.

Connelly, F. M., & Clandinin, D. J. (2006). Narrative inquiry. In J. L. Green, G. Camilli, & P. Elmore (Eds.), *Handbook of complementary methods in education research* (3rd ed., pp. 477–487). Mahwah, NJ: Lawrence Erlbaum.

Dick, P. (2004). Discourse analysis. In C. Cassell, & G. Symon (Eds.), *Essential guide to qualitative methods in organizational research* (pp. 203–213). Thousand Oaks, CA: Sage.

Doyle, J. (2019). Harassment and the privilege of unknowing: The case of Larry Nassar. *Differences – A Journal of Feminist Cultural Studies,* 30(1). Retrieved from https://escholarship.org/uc/item/3389s08d

Dwyer, C. (2019, September 5). Michigan State University to pay $4.5 million fine over Larry Nassar scandal. *NPR.* Retrieved from https://www.npr.org/2019/09/05/757909245/michigan-state-university-to-pay-4-5-million-fine-over-larry-nassar-scandal

Foss, S. (2018). *Rhetorical criticism: Exploration and practice* (5th ed.). Long Grove, IL: Waveland Press.

Frey, L. R., Botan, C. H., & Kreps, G. L. (2000). *Investigating communication: An introduction to research methods* (2nd ed.). Englewood Cliffs, NJ: Prentice Hall.

Gabriel, Y., & Griffiths, D. S. (2004). Stories in organizational research. In C. Cassell, & G. Symon (Eds.), *Essential guide to qualitative methods in organizational research* (pp. 114–126). Thousand Oaks, CA: Sage.

Gerdes, K. (2019). Trauma, trigger warnings, and the rhetoric of sensitivity. *Rhetoric Society Quarterly,* 49(1), 3–24.

Gibson, K. L. (2021). A rupture in the courtroom: Collective rhetoric, survivor speech, and the subversive limits of the victim impact statement. *Women's Studies in Communication,* 44(4), 518–554.

Glenn, C. (2004). *Unspoken: A rhetoric of silence.* Carbondale, IL: Southern Illinois University Press.

Harris, K. L. (2019). *Beyond the rapist: Title IX and sexual violence on US campuses.* New York: Oxford University Press.

Hartley, J. (2004). Case study research. In C. Cassell, & G. Symon (Eds.), *Essential guide to qualitative methods in organizational research* (pp. 323–333). Thousand Oaks, CA: Sage.

Kesto, K., Chang, S., LaSata, K., & Hoadley, J. (2018, April 5). *Letter to the Michigan House of Representatives.* Retrieved from https://www. wlns.com/news/house-lawmakers-reveal-details-of-investigation-into-msu-involving-larry-nassar/amp/

"Key Terms and Phrases." *RAINN.* Retrieved from https://www.rainn. org/articles/key-terms-and-phrases

Kozlowski, K. (2018, January 19). What MSU knew: 14 were warned of Nassar abuse. *The Detroit News.* Retrieved from https://www. detroitnews.com/story/tech/2018/01/18/msu-president-told-nassar-complaint-2014/1042071001/

Kozlowski, K. (2021, December 21). Court vacates conviction of former MSU gymnastics coach Kathie Klages. *The Detroit News.* Retrieved from https://www.detroitnews.com/story/news/local/michigan/2021/12/21/kathie-klages-larry-nassar-conviction-vacated-lying-to-police-michigan-state-university/8985174002/

Kwiatkowski, M., Alesia, M., & Evans, T. (2016, August 4). A blind eye to sex abuse: How USA Gymnastics failed to report cases. *IndyStar.* Retrieved from https://www.indystar.com/story/news/investigations/2016/08/04/usa-gymnastics-sex-abuse-protected-coaches/85829732/

LaFrance, M., & Nicolas, M. (2012). Institutional ethnography as materialist framework for writing program research and the faculty-staff work standpoints project. *College Composition and Communication,* 64 (1), 130–150.

Mack, J. (2019, January 29). Ex-MSU president Lou Anna Simon arraigned on charges in perjury case. *mLive.* Retrieved from https://www.mlive. com/news/2018/11/ex-msu_president_lou_anna_simo_2.html

McCray, K. L. (2015). Intercollegiate athletes and sexual violence: A review of literature and recommendations for future study. *Trauma, Violence, & Abuse,* 16(4), 438–443.

Porter, J. E., Sullivan, P., Blythe, S., Grabill, J. T., & Miles, L. (2000). Institutional critique: A rhetorical methodology for change. *College Composition and Communication,* 51(4), 610–642.

Propen, A. D., & Schuster, M. L. (2010). Understanding genre through the lens of advocacy: The rhetorical work of the victim impact statement. *Written Communication,* 27(1) 3–35.

Pucin, D. (2008, July 23). Moceanu accuses Karolyis of abuse. *Los Angeles Times.* Retrieved from https://www.latimes.com/archives/la-xpm-2008-jul-23-sp-karolyi23-story.html

Ryan, J. (2018). *Little girls in pretty boxes: The making and breaking of elite gymnasts and figure skaters.* New York: Grand Central Publishing.

Smagorinsky, P. (2008). The method section as conceptual epicenter in constructing social science research reports. *Written Communication,* 25(3), 389–411.

Stenberg, S. J. (2022). Acknowledging betrayal: The rhetorical power of victim impact statements in the Nassar hearing. *Rhetoric Review,* 41(1), 45–58.

Ungerleider, S., & Ulich, D. (Producers), & Carr, E. L. (Director) (2019). *At the heart of gold: Inside the USA Gymnastics scandal* [Motion picture]. United States: HBO.

U.S. Senate (2019, July). *The courage of survivors: A call to action.* U.S. Senate Report, Washington, DC.

"Victim impact statements" (2020). *The United States Attorney's Office, District of Alaska.* Retrieved from https://www.justice.gov/usao-ak/victim-impact-statements

"Who Is Larry Nassar?" *Lansing State Journal.* Retrieved from https://www.lansingstatejournal.com/pages/interactives/larry-nassar-timeline/

Yin, R. (1994). *Case study research: Design and methods* (2nd ed.). Thousand Oaks, CA: Sage.

4   Victims' voices

Larry Nassar worked at Michigan State University (MSU) and with USA Gymnastics (USAG) for decades and also volunteered to treat injured gymnasts at Gedderts' Twistars USA Gymnastics Club in Dimondale, Michigan. Nassar practiced osteopathic medicine and performed osteopathic manipulation, a technique where a doctor uses his or her hands to move a patient's muscles and joints to stretch them by applying gentle pressure and resistance (Adams, 2018). Specifically, Nassar claimed to specialize in pelvic floor physical therapy, which he presented to his victims as an "unconventional" treatment for curing their pain, even if the injury was nowhere near their pelvis. Roni Caryn Rabin (2018) writes that pelvic floor physical therapy is an actual treatment that "uses internal vaginal soft tissue manipulation, or massage, to relieve pelvic pain by accessing muscles that cannot be reached any other way." However, this is not the first line of treatment for the types of sports injuries Nassar treated, and Nassar was not certified in pelvic floor physical therapy. Even in the face of criminal prosecution, Nassar maintained that his "treatments" were legitimate medical procedures (Adams, 2018). Nassar digitally penetrated his patients vaginally and anally without wearing gloves and generally without their consent. He was also accused of inappropriate touching, such as fondling his patients' breasts during various treatments. Most of Nassar's victims were minors, and in many cases the victims' parents were in the room during the treatments but unaware of what Nassar was truly doing. In other cases, such as at Twistars and during the national team training camps, Nassar was permitted to perform these "treatments" on minors unsupervised and without parental consent.

DOI: 10.4324/9781003349846-4

In November 2017, Nassar entered into a plea agreement on state charges of multiple counts of criminal sexual conduct in Eaton and Ingham Counties in Michigan. During his trial in Ingham County, Nassar pleaded guilty to seven counts of first-degree criminal sexual conduct with minors under the age of 16 that occurred in Ingham County. During the Eaton County trial, Nassar pleaded guilty to three counts of criminal sexual conduct that occurred at Twistars USA Gymnastics Club between September 2009 and September 2011. As part of the plea agreement in both trials, Judge Rosemarie Aquilina (Ingham County) and Judge Janice K. Cunningham (Eaton County) allowed all survivors who wished to present victim impact statements to the Court during the sentencing hearings. Judge Aquilina said in *At the Heart of Gold* that "[Nassar's] attorneys asked if I would take a plea, and I advised, 'That's fine, but I'm going to let everybody talk.' Because he harmed so many, not just the girls, but everybody who touches this case" (HBO, 2019, 58:39). In all, 204 victims presented statements between the two hearings. Some victims presented in person or by video, while others submitted written statements to be read by court officials or family.

Analysis of victim impact statements

As outlined in Chapter 3, I conducted a narrative theme analysis of 192 victim impact statements from the sentencing hearings in Eaton and Ingham Counties, representing a total of 181 individual victims' voices. (My criteria for including and excluding impact statements for this study are discussed in Chapter 3.) All victims included were women who participated in gymnastics, cheerleading, dance, or figure skating and/or were athletes for MSU. The comprehensive list of themes identified (100 in total) is provided in Table 4.1. Themes are grouped into five main narrative categories: (1) ethos of Larry Nassar at the time of abuse, (2) reasons for speaking/not speaking about abuse, (3) reasons for speaking at the sentencing hearing, (4) consequences of abuse, and (5) institutional culture. Findings in each of these five categories are presented in the following sections.

Table 4.1 Themes analyzed by category

Category	Theme
1 Ethos of Larry Nassar at time of abuse	1 Trust in Nassar as a person 2 Trust in Nassar as a medical professional 3 Felt lucky/privileged to be treated by Nassar 4 Nassar was "the nice guy," a friend/confidant, a protector, a gift giver 5 Reference to gymnastics memorabilia in Nassar's office 6 Reference to Nassar's fame/reputation 7 Felt Nassar truly cared about them 8 Nassar had a personal relationship with the victim and/or parents
2 Reasons for speaking/not speaking about abuse	9 Nassar's reputation 10 Wouldn't be believed or listened to/would be ridiculed 11 Didn't feel they could contradict the expert (e.g., who was I to question it?) 12 Afraid to be rude, disobedient, or upsetting to Nassar 13 Consequences in sport 14 Had no other choice than to see Nassar 15 Would make you weird/different 16 Feeling of being in denial/repressing feelings about Nassar and/or his treatments 17 Feelings of powerlessness/vulnerability 18 Nassar's ability to lie/manipulate 19 Vulnerability of being a child 20 Complying with coach for fear of losing place on team/losing dream 21 Thought it must be legitimate "treatment" and/or would make them feel better 22 Willing to do anything to get better/get back to sport 23 Winning was all that mattered 24 Knew it was sexual assault but did not speak up 25 Saw signs of abuse (e.g., Nassar had an erection, wouldn't perform procedure with medical students in room, asked to remove clothing)

26 Parent(s) supported Larry Nassar
27 Coach(es) supported Larry Nassar
28 Community supported Larry Nassar
29 Too uncomfortable/didn't know how to explain it/felt humiliated
30 Thought parents knew/parent was in the room
31 Told parent(s)
32 Told other teammates/asked teammates about procedure/reassured by others
33 Did speak up but had other consequences
34 Did speak up but was not believed/no action taken
35 Too young to understand what sex/sexual abuse was
36 Inability to recognize/speak up about abuse because of sport training culture
37 Did not recognize the "treatment" as sexual assault until the *IndyStar* article was published/others spoke out publicly
38 Fear or hesitation for their story to be public, felt "stupid," or feared other consequences if identified
39 Did not know how to report it

3 Reasons for speaking at the sentencing hearing

40 Encouraged by/found strength from other survivors' testimony
41 Survivor voices deserve to be heard
42 Never wanted it to happen again
43 Felt like voice needed to be heard by/for other victims
44 Did it for their own child(ren)
45 Wanted to do the right thing, encourage change
46 Did it for their own healing
47 Wanted closure
48 Motivated by anger/hatred for Nassar
49 Wanted justice/maximum sentence for Nassar
50 Wanted justice for MSU/USAG/Twistars/other enablers
51 Motivated by Nassar's Letter to Judge Aquilina
52 Needed to forgive Nassar

(Continued)

Category	Theme
4 Consequences of abuse	53 Uncomfortable during "treatments"
	54 Experienced extreme fear or pain during "treatments"
	55 Feelings of shame, violation, dirtiness, and/or self-hatred
	56 Blamed self for abuse
	57 Feelings of powerlessness
	58 Loss of "innocence"
	59 Self-harm, suicidal thoughts, and/or attempted suicide
	60 Need to be in control of situations
	61 Trouble with intimacy
	62 Inability to see male doctors
	63 Lack of success in sport/had to quit
	64 Inability to trust/see health care providers
	65 Inability to trust men
	66 Inability to trust anyone
	67 PTSD, anxiety, depression, or other mental health consequences
	68 Inability to perform at job or school
	69 Parents' shame, regret, and/or guilt
	70 Feelings of betrayal and/or anger at MSU/USAG/Twistars/other enablers
	71 Feeling of betrayal by and/or hatred/ anger toward Nassar
	72 Anger at being silenced
	73 Nassar intentionally misdiagnosing/ mishandling to keep in his care
	74 Not healing properly because focus was on getting back to training faster
	75 Guilt for not realizing it was abuse and/or speaking out sooner
	76 Guilt for telling/allowing other athletes to see Nassar
	77 Loved ones not willing to talk about abuse/difficult to discuss with loved ones
	78 Fear for own children around others/ being abused
	79 Negative impact on relationships
	80 Other physical impacts
	81 Sleeplessness
	82 Financial loss

5 Institutional culture

83 Strength of survivors because they are/were athletes
84 Sport as an environment of fear/stress/anxiety
85 Coach was physically or mentally abusive
86 Sport was "my life," defined me
87 Team was family
88 Multiple repeated injuries
89 Training in constant pain
90 Inability to speak about concerns or question coach/authority
91 Pain and physical discomfort were normal
92 Coach/institution was not protecting safety and health of athletes
93 Separation of body/skill from self
94 Different rules apply to athletes
95 Body overly scrutinized/disordered eating, issues with body image
96 Nassar had too much power/access
97 Feelings of exploitation
98 Money/reputation was more important than people
99 Separation of parents from athletes
100 Proper procedures not followed for consent, wearing gloves, parental guidance, etc.

Category 1: Ethos of Larry Nassar

Figure 4.1 provides the overall distribution of victim testimony within the five narrative categories.

For me, perhaps the most unexpected outcome of this analysis was how often the victims referenced Nassar's fame and reputation and just how large a role Nassar's ethos as a doctor appeared to play in the victims' experiences, including their hesitation/inability to speak up about abuse. Frequent themes in the testimony related to the ethos of Larry Nassar at the time of his abuse included victims' trust in Nassar as a person or as a medical professional, feelings of luck/privilege to be treated by Nassar, various references to Nassar's fame and reputation, feelings that Nassar truly cared about his victims, and statements that Nassar had established a personal relationship

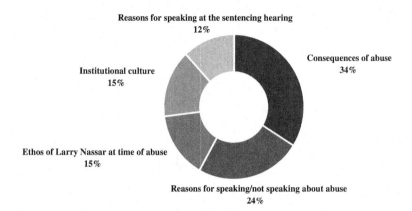

Reasons for speaking at the sentencing hearing
12%

Consequences of abuse
34%

Institutional culture
15%

Ethos of Larry Nassar at time of abuse
15%

Reasons for speaking/not speaking about abuse
24%

Figure 4.1 Distribution of victim testimony within narrative categories.

with the victim and/or her family. Figure 4.2 portrays the number of mentions for each of the eight themes included in this category.

Trust in Larry Nassar was a frequently cited reason for complying with his "treatments," though that trust came from two distinct sources. Nearly 30 percent of victims expressed trust in Larry Nassar as a person, often because of his friendly and seemingly caring personality or because they and/or their families had established personal relationships with Nassar. Nassar would give his victims gifts as part of their "grooming," whereby a perpetrator gradually gains a child's trust with the intent of sexual abuse (Pollack, 2015). Nassar gave Victim 210 a plush rhino signed by Nastia Liukin, her favorite gymnast. He gave Emily Morales a 2012 Olympic tea towel from London with all of the women's gymnastics team's signatures on it. Dozens of victims recalled how he gave them Olympic pins, autographed photos from famous gymnasts, water bottles, shirts, backpacks, and more. Nassar won over his victims' families as well. Victim 210's father would buy Nassar his favorite Colombian cigars and text him about non-medical topics. Taylor Cole's mother would bring Nassar pumpkin muffins as a thank you. According to his victims, Nassar leveraged his ability to be the "nice guy" against the backdrop of intense, physically and mentally draining, and sometimes abusive sports training. In particular, gymnasts at Gedderts' Twistars USA Gymnastics Club, where Nassar volunteered on Monday nights, claimed that Nassar was a welcome escape from the physically and verbally abusive coaching of owner John Geddert. Bailey Lorencen said:

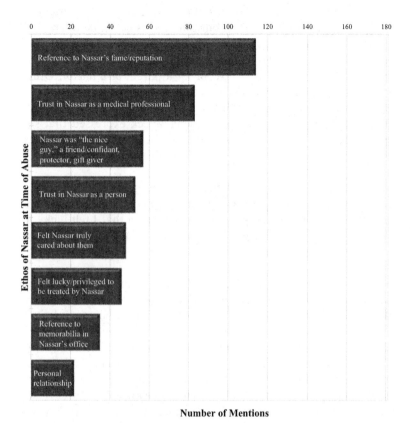

Figure 4.2 Mentions of themes in category 1.

It's clear that in an environment like Twistars a monster like the defendant could thrive. He just had to be the nice guy so that all these young girls would look at him as the savior. This was the tactic he used.

In all, nearly one-third of the victims made reference in their impact statements to Larry Nassar being "the nice guy," a friend/confidant, a protector, and/or a gift giver.

Approximately 46 percent of victims stated that they trusted Larry Nassar because he was a medical professional. Unfortunately, Nassar's profession meant that many of the girls and women who walked through his door had already been taught by their parents or culturally conditioned to trust him because he was a doctor, even if he had to access sensitive areas of their bodies. "Throughout our society, we are taught to trust our doctors," said Annette Hill. At doctor's appointments with my own children, for example, the doctor has frequently reiterated that nobody should be looking at or touching their private areas except for a parent *or a doctor.* Other victims were told repeatedly by their coaches and other adults in their lives to trust Nassar because he was "the best" doctor for treating their injuries. For example, Helena Wieck expressed that she trusted Nassar not only because he was a doctor, but also because of his reputation within the gymnastics community. She stated:

> I could not fathom that someone I was taught to trust, a doctor, could intentionally harm me. In the gymnastics community, Nassar is seen as a highly skilled physician that I felt lucky to be able to go see. He was always recommended to me. He was always respected, and he was fully trusted.

Victim 163 felt she could not contradict a medical professional and was therefore unable to recognize the abuse. "We had no right to think that what he was doing was wrong. I mean, he was a doctor, and I've always had an immense amount of respect for doctors," she said. Their trust in Nassar as a doctor made it difficult not only for victims to refuse Nassar's "treatments," but also made them less likely to question or report his abuse. "In hindsight, what he did made me feel so uncomfortable, and he was a doctor and everybody said he was great so I convinced myself it was okay for years and years and years because of that," said Lyndsy Gamet/Carr. Since trust in medical professionals is a more universal norm, the victims' trust in Nassar as a doctor is one factor in not reporting abuse that was not necessarily determined by the victims' age, training culture, or sport played. (Important exceptions to implicit trust in medical authority should be noted, however, such as transgender people and fat people, who often must be prepared to challenge bias or navigate misdiagnosis from their medical providers. These communities can offer insight into issues of patient self-advocacy.)

Most notably, however, nearly two-thirds of the victims referenced Nassar's fame or reputation in their impact statements, making it the second most cited theme at the sentencing hearings revealed in my analysis. Amy Labadie suggested that both his ethos as a doctor and his celebrity status helped Nassar deceive his victims, stating that: "Doctors of his highest stature and any doctor are to be inherently trusted. I now realize this level of celebrity status was a strong basis for his manipulation." Of note, nearly one in five victims referenced the gymnastics memorabilia on the walls of Nassar's office at MSU, including signed pictures and thank you notes from Olympians. Larissa Boyce recalled:

> I remember feeling awestruck at my first appointment with you as I looked at all the pictures on the walls of you and the gymnasts I idolized... I could not believe how lucky I was to have the privilege of seeing you. You were the one who helped Kerri Strug after her injury at the 1996 Olympics.

Even Nassar's physical space was designed to capitalize on his celebrity status, as well as his victims' tendencies to idolize their sports heroes. Nassar's celebrity status as a world-renowned gymnastics doctor was one of the most common reasons his victims cited for not questioning his procedures and speaking up about their experiences. More than one-fourth of the victims stated that they felt lucky or privileged to be treated by Nassar because of his reputation. "Having Larry at our disposal for our injuries was almost an honor," said Clasina Syrovy. "We all thought how lucky we are to have him available to go see. He was world-renowned. Everyone in the gymnastics community knew Larry. He is or was the guru of sports medicine for our sport." As I stated in Chapter 2, fame matters in the sports world. Achieving fame is a goal of playing sports and a value for most athletes. It is clear from the victims' statements that Nassar leveraged his fame expertly to build a reputation that would not be questioned and would allow him to abuse his patients without consequence.

Category 2: Reasons for speaking/not speaking about abuse

During the victim impact statements at both hearings, most victims addressed, in some form, their reason(s) for either telling others about the abuse or for keeping it to themselves. As shown in Figure 4.1, themes related to the victims' reasons for speaking or not speaking about their abuse had the second most frequent number of mentions (behind consequences of abuse). I cannot say definitively why so many victims felt they needed to address the question of why they did not speak up sooner, as this was not an expected requirement of the victim impact statements. However, multiple victims did mention the public's and even their loved ones' frequent questioning of their motives and timing in speaking up. For example, Bailey Lorencen did not mince words in addressing critics:

> I have had people close to me ask me why I never told anyone or act surprised or confused that no one ever spoke up. Do you

know what that's like to be asked questions like this? To those people I want to say, how dare you. How dare you have the audacity to ask anyone such a shaming question. No one ever has the right to ask a victim of sexual abuse why they never said anything. Unless it happened to you, have the common sense to know it is none of your business. Unless it happened to you, you probably wouldn't understand anyways.

As a researcher, I have fully noted Lorencen's perspective and will not speculate here beyond suggesting that victims may have felt the need to address this question in response to the public's fascination and (uninformed) opinions related to a highly publicized case. Nearly 15 percent of the victims expressed fear or hesitation for their story to be public, many because they feared the public would think they were "stupid" for not recognizing the abuse and speaking up sooner or feared other consequences from the public; from their employers; or even from their friends, teammates, and family members. As Jennifer Doyle (2019) argues in her study of Amanda Thomashow's Title IX complaint:

> The narratives of Nassar's victims take on the form of crises of knowing—of feeling stupid/not stupid—a feeling that also revolves around the difficulty of squaring their sense of what was happening with the shame of being the subject who names his conduct as sexual.
>
> (p. 36)

And it turns out that, even when Nassar's victims faced the shame and consequences of speaking up, institutions and enablers were ignoring victims' complaints for a very long time.

As we now know, multiple victims did actually report Nassar over the years, but no action was taken against him. Just a few of these reports included:

- In 1997, Larissa Boyce reported Nassar to MSU's women's gymnastics coach Kathie Klages, who dissuaded her from filing a report.
- In 2000, Tiffany Thomas Lopez notified MSU personnel, only to be ignored.
- In 2004, Brianne Randall filed a police report in Meridian Township that had no results.

- In 2014, Amanda Thomashow filed a Title IX complaint that was poorly managed and resulted in a finding of no wrongdoing.
- In 2015, Aly Raisman and McKayla Maroney told an investigator working for USAG that Nassar had abused them (Brody, 2018).

Victim 55 said during the sentencing hearing in Ingham County that she did tell a coach on the gymnastics team at MSU about Nassar's abuse, but that Kathie Klages "chose to put Larry's name, her identity, and the university's reputation above the choice to protect me." Victim 55 told the Court:

My concerns and fears were minimized by those in authority positions at MSU. … I was a child. I did my best, and I did speak up. Even if I said it louder or more often, it wouldn't have mattered because we can see now that many girls and women spoke to people in authority at MSU and they were not heard.

In all, 12 victims claimed in their victim impact statements that they did speak up about the abuse but were not believed, no action was taken, and/or they experienced other consequences, and 8 victims said they had told their parents about the abuse. Those who did not speak up about the abuse pointed to a number of explanations. Figure 4.3 portrays the number of mentions for the top ten themes included in this narrative category.

The most frequently cited theme in this analysis across all narrative categories was the vulnerability of being a child. Around 69 percent of victims pointed to the vulnerability of being a child as a reason for not speaking up about Nassar's abuse. Nassar abused children as young as 6 years old. Of the victims whose age at first abuse was available to me, the average age was approximately 13 years old. "I was so young and naïve," said Meaghan Ashcraft. "I had no idea what this monster was doing to me." Nearly 23 percent of victims stated that they were too young to understand what sex or sexual abuse was and therefore did not report their experiences.

Kassie Castle stated that, at just 12 years old, she did not know if the bleeding caused by Nassar's "treatments" was from menstruation, even though she was bleeding anally. She said: "I complained to my mother about bleeding. Being so young, I did not know if it were lady issues or not. It definitely was not. I was rectally bleeding and shortly after I discovered a hemorrhoid." Some victims stated

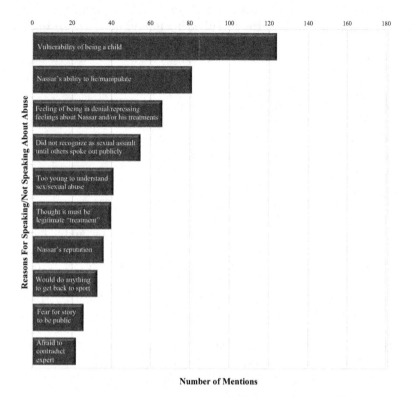

Figure 4.3 Mentions of most common themes in category 2.

that, because they were so young, they could not find the words or were too embarrassed to talk to their parents about what happened with Nassar, even if they felt like something was wrong. "I was so young, I did not even know what my body was," said Madison Bonofiglio. "I was so young, innocent, trusting, and saw the best in people." According to the victims, Nassar manipulated this youthful innocence, trust, and vulnerability expertly. It is therefore unsurprising that one of the most frequently mentioned themes was Larry Nassar's ability to lie and manipulate his victims (about 45 percent). The girls were simply doing what they were told and trusting their doctor to make them better.

Particularly with elite athletes, the training and conditioning that lead to making athletes "coachable" and separating their ability from their "self" usually begin in adolescence. The rhetorical aspects of athletic training with young athletes efface the *child-ness* of the child for the sake of athletic achievement and, often, to live up to adult expectations. Children are thrust into adult roles in highly competitive athletic training, and this conditioning over time contributes to an unwillingness or inability to speak up about abuse. I question whether children in these circumstances possess rhetorical agency—whether they can speak and be heard at all. Marci Hamilton, a child health and safety advocate, puts it well in *At the Heart of Gold*: "Adults prefer and protect adults. We say we protect children, but children are second-class citizens. They don't vote, they don't have power, and it's so much easier to let a child's needs go" (HBO, 2019, 36:45). I find this power differential reflected in the overwhelming number of victims who pointed to the vulnerability of being a child in living up to their coaches' expectations and complying with Nassar's treatments. They reported being afraid of disappointing the adults in their lives who expected them to act like adults. They were afraid of losing their dreams if they disobeyed their coaches. And they were afraid that they would not be believed or listened to if they spoke up because they were "just kids." In the words of Victim 178: "We were merely kids. We were scared, and we didn't have a voice."

Another unique aspect of this sexual assault case is that many victims did not realize they had been sexually assaulted until they either read the *IndyStar* news reporting on USAG or heard other public accounts about Nassar. Nearly one-third of the victims said in their impact statements that they did not recognize Nassar's "treatment" as sexual assault until the *IndyStar* article was published or others spoke out publicly about the abuse. Kristen Thelen said:

> I remember reading the *IndyStar* article and finally at 27 years old being overcome with emotion as I realized that he had touched me not for the reasons he claimed at the time but for his own twisted sexual reasons.

Morgan Margraves told about her boyfriend forwarding her a link to the *IndyStar* article. She said:

> My heart sinks to the very bottom of my stomach. A decade later and now I find out I've been molested. It's quite a surreal feeling to find out after so much time has passed that you were taken advantage of.

Christina Barba told a similar story:

> I read an article by *ESPN* about a woman with a pseudonym
> name named Jamie and the tears started falling as I read
> because her story was almost identical to mine. Somehow,
> I needed someone else to point out to me that what happened
> was abuse because I couldn't see it for myself until then. Maybe
> I just wasn't ready to see.

In statements like these from Thelen, Margraves, Barba, and many
others, in a very unusual aspect of this case, victims did not identify themselves as victims until years, even decades, after the crime,
and their triggering point was the news coverage. Some victims
stated that they had suspicions about Nassar but they did not want
to believe they had been a victim of sexual assault. However, they
could no longer deny what had actually happened to them after
listening to so many victims describe the same experiences they
endured. More than one-third of the victims expressed feelings of
being in denial or repressing feelings about Nassar and/or his treatments, and 22 percent said that, at the time, they thought it must be
legitimate "treatment" and/or would make them feel better.

Other victims pointed to a sports training culture that dissuaded
or prevented victims from speaking up. At the sentencing hearing
in Ingham County, when Clasina Syrovy addressed Larry Nassar
directly, she asked him rhetorically how his secret had been kept
for so long. When reflecting on this question herself, the only
answer that made sense to Syrovy was that Nassar was able to use
his fame to prey on athletes pre-conditioned to not speak up about
their concerns. "As a competitive gymnast, we are trained to hide
emotion, to control our feelings, and keep a level head, show no
fear," said Syrovy. About 10 percent of the victims indicated that
they were unable to recognize or speak up about abuse because of
their sport training culture. "I have been told throughout my elite
gymnastics career to not question authority as it was disrespectful,
and I was told not to speak up. Therefore, I felt like I didn't have a
voice," said Isabell Hutchins. Jeanette Antolin likewise suggested
that her elite gymnastics training ensured that she would not speak
up. "I was raised in the culture of gymnastics where we were taught
your voice doesn't matter. You follow instructions and never complain, especially about treatment," said Antolin. Many victims felt
pressure from coaches to return to training quickly or were desperate themselves to get back to the sport they loved. More than 18

percent of the victims stated that, at the time they saw Nassar, they were willing to do anything to get better or get back to their sport.

Finally, Nassar's reputation also appeared to play a role in victims' willingness to report abuse. Nearly one in five victims expressed that they were hesitant or fearful to report the abuse because of Nassar's reputation. Approximately 12 percent of the victims said that they did not feel they could contradict the expert, frequently repeating the phrase "who was I to ....?" I give just a few examples here, with emphasis added. Sarah Allen said, "It was weird and awkward, but he did it to all my teammates, so *who was I* to say it was not a correct procedure?" Reflecting on Nassar's request for her to wear "accessible" clothing to appointments, Katie Black said, "It felt a little strange having to wear a specific thing to a doctor, but *who was I* to judge his methods?" Tiffany Dutton said of the treatments, "It was uncomfortable and terrifying, but *who was I* to question the treatment that was supposed to heal me?" Referencing Nassar's reputation, Marta Stern said, "*Who was I* to question a world-renowned physician that had treated so many of my favorite Olympic gymnasts?" I find in this frequently repeated phrase not only a reflection of the power differential evident between Nassar and the patients he treated, but also further evidence of the role that Nassar's fame and reputation played in silencing his victims.

Category 3: Reasons for speaking at the sentencing hearing

At the beginning of Larry Nassar's sentencing hearing in Ingham County, 88 victims were slated to give their victim impact statements. By the final day, 156 victims had come forward to offer statements, many agreeing to be publicly identified for the first time. During their statements, many victims discussed their motivations for coming forward to face Nassar and/or what changed their minds to no longer remain silent. Figure 4.4 portrays the number of mentions for the top ten themes included in this narrative category.

It is important to note my criteria for identifying a mention as "a reason" for choosing to speak at the sentencing hearing. I did not record a theme in this category as mentioned unless the victim specifically identified this theme as a motivation to come forward and speak about the abuse at the sentencing hearing. For example, most of the victims asked the Court to give Larry Nassar the maximum sentence possible under the plea agreement. Such a request or recommendation for sentencing is typical for a victim impact

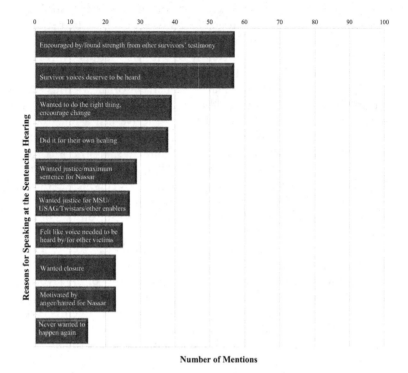

Figure 4.4 Mentions of most common themes in category 3.

statement. However, I did not code that mention under the theme of "wanted justice/maximum sentence for Nassar" unless the victim specifically expressed that this goal was a reason for choosing to speak at the sentencing hearing.

Nearly one-third of the victims expressed that they were encouraged to come forward or found the strength to speak up because of other victims' testimony. For example, Melissa Vigogne spoke of the courage she found through the voices of her sister survivors:

> I wish I had come out unscathed from my encounters with Larry and that I weren't part of this army of survivors. Yet, it is an army that I am so proud of and inspired by each and every day. One that gives me hope, and one that has helped me go from feeling powerless to powerful. That is helping me find purpose, a voice, and a battle cry. And one that helped me be here today.

Gabriela Ralph likewise thanked her fellow survivors "whose voices empowered me and helped me find my own." About 10 percent of the victims referred to the "army" or the "army of survivors" that had risen up against Nassar. "After listening to the army of women speak before me, they have given me the courage to truly say what I need to say," said Whitney Mergens. Rhetorically, the term "army of survivors" is intriguing, as it seems to have given many of the victims an avenue for both shared identity and shared purpose in managing the aftermath of abuse, while also encouraging previously silenced women to speak up. After Rachael Denhollander (the first victim to come forward publicly with accusations against Nassar after being inspired by the *IndyStar* report) finished her impact statement in Ingham County, Judge Aquilina told her "you didn't just build a file, you built an army of survivors, and you are its five-star general." Metaphorically, the comparison of the survivors to an "army" suggests a combative purpose, and Nassar's survivors have found a common purpose in coming together to fight not only Nassar but also the larger issue of sexual abuse and believing victims when they speak up. Amanda Thomashow, who had filed an unsuccessful Title IX complaint against Nassar, told him at the sentencing hearing that "you might have broken us, but from this rubble we will rise as an army of female warriors who will never let you or any man drunk off of power get away with such evil ever again." Grace French, along with other victims, helped create an organization called The Army of Survivors that provides resources, advocacy, and education to victims of sexual violence. On their website, www.thearmyofsurvivors.org, the "Force Behind the Army of Survivors" reads:

> As survivors of sexual abuse, our founders were joined together through incredibly traumatic circumstances. They lifted each other up in their darkest moments, and now they want to be the support all survivors of sexual assault and abuse desperately need.

At the sentencing hearings, victims exhibited a great concern for their fellow survivors and for other assault victims when offering reasons for speaking up. Other common themes related to the victims' reasons for speaking at the sentencing hearing included feeling that survivor voices need to be heard (31 percent), wanting to do the right thing and encourage change (22 percent), and feeling that their voice needed to be heard by/for other victims (14 percent).

When #MeToo began going viral as a social media hashtag in 2017, one goal was not only to give victims a sense of the magnitude of sexual assault and harassment but also an affirmation that survivors are not alone. There is a silence-combating property to shared experience. We have seen this phenomenon in the recent criminal cases against Harvey Weinstein, Bill Cosby, and other perpetrators of sexual violence, where victims found the strength to speak up against their abusers in numbers. In the case of Larry Nassar, victims likewise found the voice to come forward and to make their names and faces public because others shared the same experiences—because others told the Court that this terrible thing had happened to them, too.

As I indicated in my discussion of victim impact statements as sites of narrative inquiry, one typical purpose of offering a victim impact statement is seeking personal recovery and/or closure. It is unsurprising, therefore, that approximately 20 percent of the victims stated that they were speaking at the sentencing hearing as part of their own personal healing process, and about 13 percent stated that they were seeking closure from Nassar's crimes. "Without this opportunity, I'm not sure I would have ever felt closure," Taylor Helber told Judge Cunningham. Victim 177 had buried any thoughts of her abuse deep inside, but she saw the sentencing hearing as an opportunity to begin her "long-delayed healing process." She told the Court that "sharing [her] story is one of the first steps." For some victims, therefore, speaking up at the sentencing hearing and facing their abuser was primarily about healing and moving forward with their lives.

Category 4: Consequences of abuse

As discussed in Chapter 3, victim impact statements are written, at least in part, to fulfill specific purposes within the criminal justice system and during a trial. Victim impact statements are meant to help the Court understand how the crime has impacted the victim emotionally, physically, and financially, as well as help the judge decide both an appropriate sentence and (if applicable) orders for the defendant to pay restitution. Based on these purposes, some expected themes for the victim impact statements during Larry Nassar's sentencing hearings included physical, emotional, and financial impacts of Nassar's abuse to the victims, as well as negative impacts on the victims' families and relationships. It is unsurprising therefore that, while the statements also covered a wide variety of additional themes, the largest percentage of themes mentioned fall within the narrative category of the consequences of abuse (see Figure 4.1).

Given the nature of the crimes, it is also unsurprising that two of the most commonly repeated themes throughout the sentencing hearings related to consequences of abuse were feelings of betrayal by and/or hatred/anger toward Nassar and feelings of betrayal and/or anger at MSU, USAG, Twistars, and other perceived enablers. Figure 4.5 portrays the number of mentions for the top ten themes included in this narrative category.

Overwhelmingly, when speaking about the consequences of abuse, victims' statements focused on physical and emotional, rather than financial, impacts. Only five victims out of 181 made reference specifically to financial loss. More than 40 percent of the victims spoke of posttraumatic stress disorder (PTSD), anxiety,

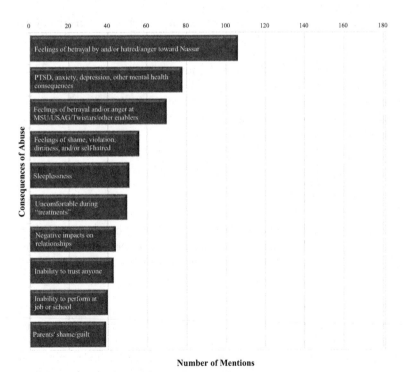

Figure 4.5 Mentions of most common themes in category 4.

depression, or other mental health consequences as a result of the abuse, and 20 percent had dealt with self-harm, suicidal thoughts, and/or attempted suicide. More than a quarter of the victims experienced sleeplessness, including insomnia, night terrors or nightmares, flashbacks, and anxiety at night. Victims also had physical consequences of Nassar's abuse, including injuries that did not heal properly as a direct result of Nassar's care. Nearly 20 percent of the victims spoke of their suspicions that Nassar had intentionally misdiagnosed their condition or mishandled their treatment to keep them in his care and maintain his access to abuse them. For instance, Jordyn Wieber questioned Nassar's treatment of her shin injuries and whether Nassar was even trying to help her pain or if he was "focused on which one of us he was going to prey on next." Danielle Moore has experienced lifelong back pain and three subsequent major surgeries in the same areas of her back that Nassar had supposedly been treating. Nearly one-third of the victims also reported feelings of shame, violation, dirtiness, and/or self-hatred as a result of the abuse they endured.

Negative impacts on the victims' families and relationships were also common themes. Nearly a quarter of the victims spoke about the negative impacts on their relationships stemming from the abuse. One common theme was shame, regret, and/or guilt experienced by the victims' parents because they did not prevent the abuse and, in many cases, were even present in the room during the abuse. For example, Jessica Howard began her statement with a story of her mother's guilt:

> I spoke with my mom last night. She is broken and blames herself. The incredible woman who sacrificed her life so I could achieve my dreams blames herself. She blames herself for not knowing there was a monster employed by USA Gymnastics. My beloved mother blames herself for not being there. When USAG, MSU, and the Olympic Committee allowed a serial predator to have free reign over its athletes, my mother is the one who blames herself.

Other frequently cited consequences to relationships included trouble with intimacy (13 percent), inability to trust men (12 percent), and inability to trust anyone (24 percent).

Three themes related to silence and silencing appeared within this narrative category. Nearly 20 percent of the victims expressed anger at being silenced by various individuals and/or institutions, including Nassar, coaches, MSU, USAG, USOPC, Twistars, and other enablers. For example, in 1997, Larissa Boyce reported Nassar's abuse to MSU Gymnastics coach Kathie Klages, but Klages (who was a personal friend of Nassar) discouraged her from filing a complaint. During the sentencing hearing, Boyce directed her anger at being silenced by both Nassar and Klages: "You and Kathie silenced me. You took away my confidence. You took away my innocence, and you took away my voice." Other victims spoke of the need to take their voices back to enact change and ensure that abuse like Nassar's never happened again. "Our silence has given the wrong people power for too long, and it is time to take our power back," said McKayla Maroney. Victims like Chelsea Williams pointed specifically to a sports training culture that conditioned victims to be silent. Speaking about elite gymnastics training culture, Williams stated:

> One of the most prevalent attitudes taught to young gymnasts engaged in the culture of gymnastics is silent suffering. From the beginning we are taught to soldier on through intense training sessions, through the emotional roller coaster of competition, through injury and fatigue, through pain. The stone faces you see on Olympic gymnasts mid-competition is as a result of this conditioning. Pain was a fact of life for me because of gymnastics, but so was silence.

Another theme related to silence was the victims' inability to speak about the abuse with their loved ones, even once they were aware of the abuse, either because the loved ones were not willing to talk about it or because the victims did not feel comfortable discussing the abuse with their loved ones. These accounts are reminiscent of other rape survivors' experiences of silencing from those around them, even close family, who are uncomfortable speaking about the assault (e.g., Raine, 1998). Along with this inability to talk with others about the abuse, many victims (about 22 percent) also expressed their own personal guilt for not realizing it was abuse and speaking up sooner.

Category 5: Institutional culture

In this final category focused on institutional culture, I listened to what victims told us *outside* of the expected functions of a victim impact statement. I listened to what the victims said about how they were talked to and treated by authority figures, how they were trained, how they perceived their role and value within the institutions, and other aspects of institutional culture. Although these mentions were not as frequent as other narrative categories, I find them particularly revealing in the context of victim impact statements. In other words, although most of these experiences did not address the specific impact of Nassar's abuse—the expected focus of the victim impact statements at his sentencing hearings— victims still felt these details were important to include to understand their experience with Nassar and within their institutions in full.

Figure 4.6 portrays the number of mentions for the top ten themes included in the narrative category of institutional culture. The highest number of mentions (approximately 40 percent) involved concerns that proper procedures were not followed during Nassar's treatments, such as the doctor wearing gloves, seeking informed consent, having a parent or other adult present in the room, etc. In

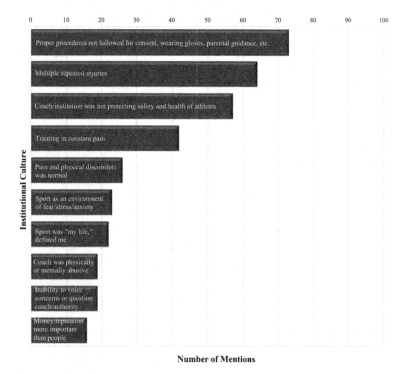

Figure 4.6 Mentions of most common themes in category 5.

particular, victims noted that Nassar did not wear gloves during the treatments, an obvious red flag and health risk when working with patients, especially internally. Nearly one-third of the victims also indicated that their coach and/or institution was not committed to protecting the health and safety of athletes, and 23 percent argued that Nassar had too much power and unfettered access to patients.

Victim D expressed her family's devastation at knowing that, during the timeframe she was assaulted, Nassar had been under investigation with no action taken or new procedures enforced to protect patients. She said:

> If one or any of the stipulations had been enforced by anyone overseeing Nassar, this would have never happened. To my knowledge, I am the first known victim after he was allowed to go back to work in July 2014. That fact is almost inconceivable to us, that he was so brazen to do the sexual assault in front of my mom, but also knowing he was still under investigation. It actually speaks volumes to what he knew he could get away with because no one was truly watching. He had mastered his performance, his act, his actions, his every move.

Victim D was referring to Amanda Thomashow's 2014 Title IX complaint against Nassar. MSU ultimately decided that Nassar's treatments were "medically appropriate," but gave a different version of the investigative report prepared in response to the Title IX claim to Thomashow than they did to Nassar (Casarez et al., 2018). In Nassar's version of the report, he was advised to revise his procedures to prevent "opening the practice up to liability [and] exposing patients to unnecessary trauma," such as adequately explaining procedures, giving patients the choice to leave their clothing on during procedures, and having a resident or nurse in the room during sensitive procedures (Casarez et al., 2018). As Victim D indicates, none of these new procedures were followed or enforced, and Nassar continued to see patients without oversight for 16 months. Jessica Tarrant's haunting words likewise paint the scope of institutional failure to protect athletes: "I wasn't even alive yet the first time [Nassar] sexually assaulted someone, and I was only one the first time it was reported." Victims' sentiments that their institutions were not protecting them and that Nassar had too much power are unsurprising given that Nassar was allowed to operate unchecked for so long on hundreds, if not thousands, of victims.

Other themes, however, offered significant insight into the training conditions and institutional cultures that not only enabled a child predator but also made athletes unwilling or unable to speak up about the abuse. As I stated previously, one uncomfortable truth about this research is that Larry Nassar had access to *so many* young athletes because *so many* young athletes were living with pain. Approximately 35 percent of the victims made reference to experiencing multiple repeated injuries in their sport, which unfortunately meant visiting Nassar frequently. I have argued previously that normalizing pain and a high risk of (often repeated) injury is one characteristic of "rhetorical cultures of champion-building." During their impact statements, nearly a quarter of the victims described training in constant pain, while nearly 15 percent spoke about pain and physical discomfort being a "normal" part of their training and sport experience. Bailey Lorencen recounted falling from the high bar directly onto her head during practice and lying on the ground in pain when her coach, John Geddert, made her get up and finish the remaining two hours of practice. Her teammates had to help her dress to go home. Later that evening, a visit to the hospital revealed that Lorencen had broken her neck in four places and was lucky not to have been paralyzed from moving on such an injury. Victim 13 was forced to compete on a torn hamstring, even though she could not even run down the vault runway. Under pressure from her coach and at Nassar's insistence that nothing was wrong with her, Isabell Hutchins endured practices and competitions with excruciating leg pain for over a month. When she finally had an x-ray performed at an emergency room, she learned that she actually had a broken leg that "looked like an axe splitting a piece of wood, and every time that I tumbled the bone splintered more and more." But not only was experiencing physical pain during and after training or competition a constant reality for many athletes, they were also trained not to show it or speak about it. Chelsea Williams offered a frightening description of her elite gymnastics training:

> I learned early on that pain was not an excuse and that it was shameful to even mention it. Pain was weakness, and so I learned to bear it for years, through injuries that woke me up at night, that throbbed so much I would mistake them for my own heartbeat, that ached so badly I felt like someone had taken a hammer to my joints. Injuries that certainly would have sounded loud, insistent alarm bells for anybody else. To ask for

help, to admit that something hurt, I had to be suffering such extreme and unmitigated pain that I could barely function.

If Williams felt powerless to speak about her pain or to ask for help with such significant suffering, it is no wonder that she did not feel empowered to speak up about Nassar's abuse.

Other frequent references to institutional culture included describing their sport training as an environment of fear/stress/anxiety (about 13 percent), describing their coach as physically or mentally abusive (about 10 percent), and expressing an inability to speak about concerns or question the coach/authority (about 10 percent). It is important to note here again that victims chose to include details about institutional culture within the context of offering victim impact statements, which have different stated purposes within the criminal justice system. The fact that many victims spoke of their experiences with institutional culture in this context suggests to me that the number of athletes enduring these conditions is likely much higher. Later in her impact statement, Williams specifically addressed public comments like why girls did not report the abuse earlier or even know it was abuse. To ask these questions still, said Williams, is to be ignorant of the situation and environment in which the abuse took place. "You have no concept of the culture of gymnastics, a culture that promotes fear of challenging authority, an environment that often breeds physical and mental abuse, and a system designed to limit parental involvement," said Williams. Though I had not yet read Williams' impact statement when I developed the characteristics of "rhetorical cultures of champion-building" (using fear and shame to motivate, separating the athlete from their tool [body] and ability [skill], normalizing pain and a high risk of injury, and intentionally separating parents from their children in athletic training), her sentiments reflect this argument well.

Nearly all of the victims who spoke about the negative consequences of sport training culture during their impact statements were elite or Olympic-level athletes and/or trained at Gedderts' Twistars USA Gymnastics Club. John Geddert, the owner and former head coach at Twistars and the 2012 head coach for the U.S. Olympic women's gymnastics team, had been under investigation since January 2018, when he was suspended by USAG. Geddert announced he was retiring days after the suspension and transferring ownership of Twistars to his wife. In February 2021, Geddert was charged with 20 counts of human trafficking and forced labor, one count of first-degree sexual assault, one count of second-degree sexual assault, racketeering, and lying to a police officer. The human trafficking charges—a creative legal strategy that may set precedent for prosecuting abusive coaches—were related to forced labor resulting in injury and human trafficking a minor for forced labor (Waller, 2021). "The victims suffer from disordered eating, including bulimia and anorexia, suicide attempts, and self-harm," said Michigan Attorney General Dana Nessel during a news conference to announce the charges. Nessel said that Geddert subjected his gymnasts to "excessive physical conditioning, repeatedly being forced to perform even while injured, extreme emotional abuse and physical abuse, including sexual assault" (Murphy & Barr, 2021). Hours after a judge issued the warrant, Geddert died by suicide.

Geddert had a long-time professional relationship and friendship with Nassar. Particularly at the Eaton County sentencing hearing, which was focused on Nassar's counts of criminal sexual conduct while he was volunteering at Twistars, many victims spoke about a training culture under Geddert that ensured they would not speak up about Nassar's abuse. "There isn't one bone in my body that doesn't hate John Geddert for everything he has done to me in my career," said Makayla Thrush during her victim impact statement, calling Geddert "one of the enablers of this disgusting monster." Thrush was a gymnast at Twistars from age 7 to 17. Describing a physically and mentally abusive training environment and an injury at Geddert's hands during an outburst of rage that ended her career, Thrush said "you told me to kill myself, not just once but many other times and, unfortunately, I let you get the best of me, because after you ended my career, I tried."

Annie Labrie was a gymnast at Twistars for her entire adolescence. In her victim impact statement, Labrie specifically called out the "gymnastics world" as a culture where a pedophile could thrive without consequences. She said:

> Our bodies did not belong to us. Our experiences, physical and emotional, were constantly invalidated, and we learned early on not to question authority, to not expect respect from men. We were, quite literally, judged for our every move. Every hair out of place, every ounce of fat carried by our over-worked muscles, the strict demand to be thin alongside the enforcement of unhealthy dieting, led to an alarming rate of disordered eating and lasting battles with body image. Coaching by fear, intimidation, shame, and explicit favoritism was the norm.

I have argued that athletic instruction is unique in that, because an athlete's "tool" is his or her body, both success and failure often involve bodily consequences. And in the elite training culture Labrie describes, the rights of the individual participant are overshadowed or even lost in the pursuit of winning. Athletes' bodies are, as Labrie states, literally not their own. And as such, their bodies were disposable. Béla Károlyi described how athletes functioned as a means to an end, saying "You were not good? Good-bye. If you goofed off once, you were out in two minutes. As a coach, I had no obligation to you" (McPhee & Dowden, 2018, p. 129). Joan Ryan (2000) calls gymnasts "disposable heroes" whose bodies belong to coaches or parents and who "know when their bodies give out, there's someone else ready to take their places" (p. 48). In this training culture, victims did not feel that they were able to speak up in defense of their own bodies for fear of losing their hope of athletic advancement.

Summary of victim impact statement analysis

This theme analysis of the victim impact statements presented at Larry Nassar's sentencing hearing in Ingham and Eaton Counties suggests a number of possible takeaways, summarized as follows:

* Nassar's ethos as a doctor played a key role in the victims' experiences, including their hesitation/inability to speak up about abuse.
* Trust in Larry Nassar was a frequently cited reason for complying with his "treatments," and that trust came from both his personal relationship as the "nice guy" and the victims' trust in a medical professional.
* Nassar's celebrity status helped him deceive his victims.
* Their trust in Nassar as a doctor and frequent references to his reputation made it difficult not only for victims to refuse Nassar's "treatments," but also made them less likely to question or report his abuse.
* Multiple victims did actually report Nassar over the years, but no action was taken against him, revealing an institutional inability/unwillingness to protect their athletes.
* The most frequently cited theme in this analysis across all narrative categories was the vulnerability of being a child. More than two-thirds of the victims pointed to the vulnerability of being a child as a reason for not questioning Nassar and/or speaking up about Nassar's abuse.

- One of the most frequently mentioned themes was Larry Nassar's ability to lie and manipulate his victims (about 45 percent).
- This sexual assault case is unique in that many victims did not realize they had been sexually assaulted until they either read the *IndyStar* news reporting on USAG or heard other public accounts about Nassar. A victim speaking up had a role in revealing the sexual abuse to hundreds of other women.
- Sports training culture played a role in dissuading or preventing victims from speaking up, including conditioning athletes to hide their feelings, never question authority, and remain silent about their physical and emotional concerns.
- Frequently repeated phrases (e.g., Who was I to question him?) during the testimony suggested a power differential between Nassar and the patients he treated.
- Victims found the voice to come forward and to make their names and faces public because others shared the same experiences. They were encouraged or found the strength to speak up because of other victims' testimony.
- In line with the purpose of victim impact statements, the largest percentage of themes mentioned fall within the narrative category of the consequences of abuse.
- Themes related to silence and silencing within the narrative category of the consequences of abuse included the victims' anger at being silenced by various individuals and/or institutions, inability to speak about the abuse with their loved ones, and guilt for not realizing it was abuse and speaking up sooner.
- Frequent sentiments were that the victims' institutions were not protecting them and that Nassar had too much power and unsupervised access to patients.
- Larry Nassar had access to so many young athletes because so many young athletes were living with pain from multiple, repeated injuries.
- Not only was experiencing physical pain during and after training or competition a constant reality for many athletes, but they were also trained not to show it or speak about it.
- Nearly all of the victims who spoke about the negative consequences of sport training culture during their impact statements were elite or Olympic-level athletes and/or trained at Gedderts' Twistars USA Gymnastics Club.
- Training in an environment of fear/stress/anxiety and with a physically and/or mentally abusive coach was a reality for many

of the victims. In this training culture, victims did not feel that they were able to speak up in defense of their own bodies.

One of my research questions asks how the rhetoric and discursive practices of youth and college athletic programs impact athletes' willingness to speak up about abuse. As explained in the previous sections, I did see evidence in the victim impact statements that rhetoric and discursive practices effectively silenced at least some of Nassar's victims, especially those athletes who trained at the elite or Olympic level and athletes who trained at Twistars. Some of these practices centered on the way athletes were trained, such as constant yelling and verbal abuse by their coaches and other aspects of what I have called "rhetorical cultures of champion-building." Jeanette Antolin was easily groomed into trusting Nassar because he was such a welcome contrast to her coach, especially when she was separated from her parents. "For a young girl away from her home being worked into exhaustion by screaming coaches, a kindly doctor offering relief from pain and a little sympathy was easy to like," said Antolin. Pain was a normal part of gymnastics training for Bailey Lorencen, whose coach "got in [her] face screaming, telling [her] to do splints on a vault runway as [she] was visibly limping from the pain." After Victim 219 injured her back on a tumbling pass, her coach yelled at her to get up and kicked her in the stomach when she said she could not move. Victim 219 said in her impact statement that, due to her coach's constant taunting and accusations that she was "being a baby," she told her parents not to attend her appointments with Nassar in the hopes that "the word would get back to my coaches that I was not a baby or a burden." Nassar began molesting her during these unsupervised visits. Because Victim 86 was "always getting screamed at, ridiculed in front of everybody at the gym, and kicked out of practice," she said in her impact statement that she "was terrified to go each day and would puke and get hives every day on [her] way to practice." It seems clear that athletes trained under such conditions would not feel empowered to speak up about Nassar's abuse and may have been less likely to recognize Nassar's treatments as abuse.

As discussed before, Nassar's reputation also appears to have played a key role in silencing victims, and I argue that, at least in part, this was due to the repeated and constantly reproduced narratives surrounding his reputation. These rhetorical practices ranged from the visual rhetoric of the memorabilia in Nassar's office to the constantly repeated catchphrases to athletes of how "lucky they were" to be seen by such a "world-renowned doctor," the "doctor to Olympians." These phrases are repeated again and again in the victim impact statements.

Analysis of victim interviews

In addition to the victim impact statements, I also analyzed two additional texts that included victim interviews, HBO's documentary *At the Heart of Gold: Inside the USA Gymnastics Scandal* and a *60 Minutes* episode on "USA Gymnastics." As rhetorical texts, I must consider that these interviews are public performances developed for specific purposes, including entertainment. While I do not doubt that the victims' statements are genuine, I needed to consider that the videos I viewed had been carefully edited and arranged to tell an editorial, dramatic, and visual "story." Because the purpose and rhetorical situation of these two texts were different from the victim impact statements, I did not include them in the same theme analysis. Instead, I analyzed them individually to determine if similar narrative threads appeared in these texts, particularly related to organization, violence, and silence.

In February 2017, CBS aired a *60 Minutes* episode in which Dr. Jon LaPook interviews former gymnasts Jeanette Antolin, Jamie Dantzscher, and Jessica Howard about their experiences with Larry Nassar and within USAG. These interviews took place nearly a year before all three women presented their victim impact statements at Larry Nassar's sentencing hearing in Ingham County. (Howard's statement was read by a court official.) At the time of the interviews, Nassar had pleaded not guilty to the charges against him in Michigan and was still defending his "treatment" as legitimate.

One narrative theme in the episode centered on an abusive training culture at the elite level within USAG, where nobody was protecting the young athletes and, as attorney John Manly put it, USAG and the Károlyis "put medals and money first" (CBS News, 2017, 7:29). Jamie Dantzscher tells Dr. LaPook that yelling and screaming were a normal part of training. When Dr. LaPook asks specifically what kinds of abusive things were said to her, Dantzscher replies, "It was never good enough. You're not good enough" (CBS News, 2017, 8:00). Jeanette Antolin then concurs that "the pressure that they put on you to be perfection for them, it was very overwhelming and stressful" (CBS News, 2017, 8:07). Again, we see that, in an environment of fear-based training and unrealistic expectations, not only could Nassar easily step in to be the "good guy," but athletes did not feel they could speak up about their concerns. If putting a toe out of line meant getting kicked off the team and losing their Olympic dream, the girls were effectively silenced. As Antolin tells Dr. LaPook, almost as if it is perfectly obvious, "you don't complain about treatment" (CBS News, 2017, 5:31).

The narrative surrounding Larry Nassar's reputation is reflected in the *60 Minutes* episode as well. Jessica Howard admits that she felt something was not right about Nassar's treatments, but she tells Dr. LaPook that she did not feel like she could say anything about it "because he was this very high-profile doctor, and I was very lucky to be at the ranch working with him" (CBS News, 2017, 5:05). Antolin likewise talks about the vulnerability of being a child and the trust that she put into Nassar and his "treatments" to make her better because he was a doctor.

HBO's documentary on USAG and Larry Nassar, *At the Heart of Gold*, offers an in-depth perspective into the Larry Nassar abuse scandal with a focus on the organizational failures of USAG. The director centers the story on various voices connected to USAG and Nassar through snippets of interviews. One longer segment in the documentary focuses on the training environment at the Károlyi's National Team Training Center in Texas, with many of the same themes repeated from the *60 Minutes* episode and the victim impact statements. In a 2018 interview for *The Washington Post*, Olympic gymnast Aly Raisman notes of her experience on the Károlyi ranch in Texas that "nobody wanted to be the one who was difficult," for fear of being cut from the team, and she looks back with anger at accepting an atmosphere that made her and her fellow gymnasts afraid to speak up about anything, even to "ask for soap" (Jenkins, 2018). Raisman directly attributes training under such conditions to making athletes more susceptible to abuse by Nassar.

In *At the Heart of Gold*, various interviewees, mostly journalists, discuss the restrictive environment at the Károlyi training camps, such as prohibiting any communication with the gymnasts' parents or personal coach, stressful and even dangerous training, severe diet restrictions, and the inability to speak up about any concerns for fear of being kicked off the team. However, Olympic gymnast Dominique Moceanu offers an interesting perspective on why the Károlyis chose Nassar, specifically, to treat the national team gymnasts. She said:

> Márta liked that Nassar would tow the company line. He would tell them exactly what they wanted to hear. There were

girls that got injured and you want to get the gymnast back? Sure, we can get her back. He would just kind of play the game because he wanted the access.

HBO (2019, 14:58)

In other words, Nassar was preferred as the team doctor because he would not make waves for the Károlyis and would get the gymnasts back to training faster. He was interested in performing his "treatments," not actually treating their injuries and insisting on proper healing protocols before the gymnasts returned to the sport. Later, in reference to her training at Twistars, Taylor Livingston suggests that gymnasts were sent to Nassar because he would give them "the shortest amount of time that could be necessary to come back from our injury," and that was the way their coach wanted it (HBO, 2019, 29:48).

One narrative theme repeated in the documentary was the normalization of pain in the sport of gymnastics. Melody Posthuma, a dancer, said "you're always told by coaches, teachers 'no pain, no gain.' So when something's painful, you're thinking this is helping me and I'm getting better because of it" (HBO, 2019, 21:09). Later, Posthuma explains the vicious cycle of constantly being in pain from training, never truly healing from Nassar's treatments, but needing to continue seeing him in the hope of feeling better. "I knew I had to go back because I needed to be relieved of my pain. So even if I hated the treatment, I would go back. And that's how so many girls were abused for so many years," said Posthuma (HBO, 2019, 25:00). The constant reality of pain and injury in gymnastics not only meant that Nassar had ample access to patients, but also that those patients would be desperate to be healed and able to get back to their sport. According to the victims, Nassar exploited this reality of gymnastics expertly.

Another long segment in the documentary is focused on John Geddert and the training environment at Twistars. When the interviewer asks Kat Ebert "Who is John Geddert?" she replies memorably: "Satan. He is, uh, the devil" (HBO, 2019, 25:59). Isabell Hutchins described her training under Geddert:

He would use more of a tactic like beating you down. He would belittle you. He would insult you, call you names. And you would feel like you weren't good enough. It was your fault you were doing things wrong.

HBO (2019, 28:22)

As mentioned before, under pressure from Geddert and at Nassar's insistence that nothing was wrong with her, Isabell Hutchins endured practices and competitions with excruciating leg pain for over a month. When she finally had an x-ray performed at an emergency room, she learned that she actually had a broken leg that looked "like a nail was hammering down" on her splintering bone from tumbling on a broken leg for so long. She tells this horrifying story in greater depth in the documentary: "Doing all the gymnastics stuff on it, it was excruciating. But a prestigious Olympic doctor is telling you nothing is wrong, so you kind of think you're crazy. I mean, it makes you wonder, what really is pain?" (HBO, 2019, 31:06). In addition to the reference to Nassar's fame, I find this last question particularly telling, as excruciating pain had become such a normal part of Hutchins' life that she could no longer grasp what pain was. This is reminiscent of Victor Vitanza's (2011) discussion of Kate Millett's *The Basement,* a disturbing story of the weeks-long torture of a young girl. Vitanza writes:

> What haunts me in *The Basement* are Millet's questions: "What is the nature of pain, or cruelty—its meaning, its essence? What does it become to the victim, to the one who inflicts it? What 'sense' does the one make to the other? What product do they produce [i.e., *make*] together?"
>
> (p. 57)

I cannot offer a philosophical answer to the nature of this product, but I contend that its consequence is silence.

Not only was experiencing physical pain during and after training or competition a constant reality for many athletes, but they were also trained not to show it or speak about it. Kristen Thelen recalls that if a girl fell at a gymnastics meet, Geddert would turn his back on her and would not watch her compete. He would also throw water bottles at gymnasts for making mistakes (HBO, 2019, 28:36). As rhetorical tactics, training techniques like yelling, belittling, name-calling, intimidation, distancing, and displays of anger send a clear message: your feelings do not matter. Suck it up. And again, Geddert's demeaning and fear-based training techniques easily set Larry Nassar up to be the "nice guy."

More than half of the documentary is focused on the institutional response to Larry Nassar (or lack thereof), which I will analyze in depth in the next chapter. However, one additional recurrent theme that appears near the end of the documentary is that many victims did not recognize Nassar's "treatments" as abuse until they read news reports or public statements. Larissa Boyce, Melody Posthuma, Taylor Livingston, Trinea Gonczar, and Jessica Ann Smith all describe the emotional consequences of hearing other victims' stories—from initial denial and disbelief to anger, horror, embarrassment, and guilt—as well as their eventual choice to speak out against Nassar. Reflecting on the victim impact statements and the many victims who ultimately decided to come forward, Morgan McCaul, a former dancer, leaves us with a sobering reminder:

> While it was very empowering to watch these women, they're taking back their voice, but they shouldn't have ever had to use it to say, "Me too." Disclosing your name and your face along with your story in this volume to be believed is a travesty.
>
> HBO (2019, 1:19:26)

How many voices were necessary to be believed? It is a difficult question indeed.

One final note I will make about the documentary is regarding the narrative weight offered to victims' voices. As I was transcribing the documentary, I noticed that a lot of the "voices" in the motion picture are not actually from Nassar's victims. Other participants included journalists who covered the story, attorneys and members of the legal teams, parents of victims, a child health and safety advocate, and so on. No doubt the production team sought these different voices to add depth and perspective to the victim interviews and overall narrative. Since I have centered this study on speaking up and listening to victims' voices, however, I was interested to determine how much of the total footage was dedicated to actual words spoken by victims. To do so, I divided my transcript into two files: victim voices and other voices. Interestingly, just slightly over half (51 percent) of the total words spoken during interviews in the film were not from Nassar's victims. I then narrowed in this comparison further to look at a specific example. At one point, Amanda Thomashow speaks about her Title IX complaint against Nassar. Recall that, in 2014, Thomashow filed a Title IX complaint after Nassar assaulted her that was poorly managed and resulted in a finding of no wrongdoing. This segment in the documentary includes back-and-forth snippets from Thomashow and her attorney, Mick Grewal. In telling Thomashow's story, Thomashow speaks a total of 131 words, and her attorney speaks 396 words. This point may seem trivial, but I find it ironic that in a documentary about victims speaking up, others are doing most of the talking for them. Have we truly listened to the lessons of Larry Nassar?

References

Adams, D. (2018, May 24). Victims share what Larry Nassar did to them under the guise of medical treatment. *IndyStar.* Retrieved from https://www.indystar.com/story/news/2018/01/25/heres-what-larry-nassar-actually-did-his-patients/1065165001/

Brody, L. (2018, October 30). The army of women who took down Larry Nassar. *Glamour.* Retrieved from https://www.glamour.com/story/women-of-the-year-2018-larry-nassar-survivors

Casarez, J., Grinberg, E., Moghe, S., & Tran, L. (2018, February 1). She filed a complaint against Larry Nassar in 2014. Nothing happened. *CNN.* Retrieved from https://www.cnn.com/2018/02/01/us/msu-amanda-thomashow-complaint-larry-nassar/index.html

CBS News (2017, February 19). *60 Minutes: USA Gymnastics* [Video file]. Retrieved from https://www.cbsnews.com/video/usa-gymnastics/

Doyle, J. (2019). Harassment and the privilege of unknowing: The case of Larry Nassar. *Differences – A Journal of Feminist Cultural Studies, 30*(1). Retrieved from https://escholarship.org/uc/item/3389s08d

Jenkins, S. (2018, March 14). Aly Raisman: Conditions at Karolyi Ranch made athletes vulnerable to Nassar. *The Washington Post.* Retrieved from https://www.washingtonpost.com/sports/olympics/aly-raisman-conditions-at-karolyi-ranch-made-athletes-vulnerable-to-nassar/2018/03/14/6d2dae56-26eb-11e8-874b-d517e912f125_story.html

McPhee, J., & Dowden, J. P. (2018). *Report of the independent investigation: The constellation of factors underlying Larry Nassar's abuse of athletes.* Boston, MA: Ropes & Gray.

Murphy, D., & Barr, J. (2021, February 25). Ex-USA Olympic gymnastics coach John Geddert faces 24 felony charges, including human trafficking, sexual assault. *ESPN.* Retrieved from https://www.espn.com/olympics/gymnastics/story/_/id/30962773/former-usa-olympics-gymnastics-coach-john-geddert-charged

Pollack, D. (2015). Understanding sexual grooming in child abuse cases. *American Bar Association.* Retrieved from https://www.americanbar.org/groups/public_interest/child_law/resources/child_law_practiceonline/child_law_practice/vol-34/november-2015/understanding-sexual-grooming-in-child-abuse-cases/

Rabin, R. C. (2018, January 31). Pelvic massage can be legitimate, but not in Larry Nassar's hands. *The New York Times.* Retrieved from https://www.nytimes.com/2018/01/31/well/live/pelvic-massage-can-be-legitimate-but-not-in-larry-nassars-hands.html

Raine, N. V. (1998). *After silence: Rape and my journey back.* New York: Three Rivers Press.

Ryan, J. (2000). *Little girls in pretty boxes: The making and breaking of elite gymnasts and figure skaters.* New York: Grand Central Publishing.

Ungerleider, S., & Ulich, D. (Producers), & Carr, E. L. (Director) (2019). *At the heart of gold: Inside the USA Gymnastics scandal* [Motion picture]. United States: HBO.

Vitanza, V. J. (2011). *Sexual violence in western thought and writing: Chaste rape.* New York: Palgrave Macmillan.

Waller, A. (2021, February 26). A gymnastics coach was charged with human trafficking. What does that mean? *The New York Times.* Retrieved from https://www.nytimes.com/2021/02/26/sports/human-trafficking-john-geddert-gymnastics.html

5   Institutions of silence

An institutional failure of USA Gymnastics (USAG) and Michigan State University (MSU), in the Nassar case and beyond, was investigating and reporting allegations of abuse to law enforcement or child protective services. This chapter examines several documents that indicate that, at an institutional level, USAG and MSU both had well-established patterns of not protecting—and silencing—their athletes.

IndyStar investigative report

The tipping point that ultimately led to Nassar's arrest, prosecution, and sentencing for criminal sexual conduct was an *IndyStar* investigative news report—but the focus of the original report was not actually Nassar. On August 4, 2016, the news outlet published "Out of Balance" by reporters Marisa Kwiatkowski, Mark Alesia, and Tim Evans, a lengthy investigation into USAG and its handling of sexual abuse complaints over decades. The story is based on records requests that *IndyStar* filed in ten states and thousands of pages of documents the reporters reviewed over four and a half months (Beggin, 2016). The story alleges that top executives at USAG, which is headquartered in Indianapolis, "failed to alert authorities to many allegations of sexual abuse by coaches—relying on a policy that enabled predators to abuse gymnasts long after USA Gymnastics had received warnings" (Kwiatkowski et al., 2016). Inspired by this original *IndyStar* report, Rachael Denhollander became the first victim to come forward publicly with accusations against Nassar, prompting a follow-up story in September 2016 that detailed Dehollander's and another Olympic gymnast's allegations against Nassar. However, perhaps now overshadowed by the subsequent intense focus on Nassar's crimes, the original *IndyStar* report suggested that a culture of sexual misconduct and failure to listen to and act on reports of abuse had permeated USAG for many years.

DOI: 10.4324/9781003349846-5

The USAG "policy that enabled predators" referenced in the quote above was what former USAG president Robert Colarossi described as "an executive policy of dismissing complaints as 'hearsay' unless they were signed by a victim or a victim's parent" (Kwiatkowski et al., 2016). Colarossi also indicated, under oath, that one purpose of the policy was preserving a coach's reputation from false allegations. Former USAG president Steve Penny also testified in 2014 that the organization feared moving forward with complaints because of the possibility of "witch hunts" against coaches. USAG seems to have been more preoccupied (bordering on paranoia) with the possibility of using sexual abuse as a retaliatory strategy in a highly competitive coaching environment than with the actual possibility that sexual abuse existed within its organization. One advocacy group representative said that USAG "errs on the side of the institution" and protecting its own reputation in handling allegations (Kwiatkowski et al., 2016). USAG has clearly not erred on the side of protecting its athletes.

For example, such a "policy" requiring that complaints be signed by a victim or a victim's parent discourages victims from reporting abuse. Courtney Kiehl, a survivor of sexual abuse by a gymnastics coach and co-founder of Abused Children Heard Everywhere Foundation, noted that since speaking up about abuse can be traumatic, victims who are reluctant to make a formal complaint might confide in a friend or trusted adult. But under USAG's policy, complaints relayed from these sources would be seen as "hearsay" and therefore not be investigated or reported to law enforcement (Kwiatkowski et al., 2016). Labeling reports not directly from victims as "hearsay" ultimately meant that USAG rarely sent complaints on to police or child protective services unless required (Kwiatkowski et al., 2016). The use of the term "hearsay" also invokes a lack of seriousness about the legitimacy of sexual abuse complaints. The *IndyStar* reported that, according to court records, from 1996 to 2006 USAG had compiled files of complaints on 54 coaches that were collecting dust in a drawer in the organization's Indianapolis executive office.

Indiana law only requires a "reason to believe" abuse has occurred to report abuse, not firsthand information, so USAG's "policy" may also have violated state law (Beggin, 2016). The *IndyStar* report outlines four of these cases of complaints against coaches that got "filed away" by USAG for years before action was taken against the sexual abusers:

- USAG received a detailed complaint in 2011 about Marvin Sharp, describing inappropriate touching of minors and warning that he should not be around children. USAG did not report Sharp to police until 4 years later when it received another allegation about Sharp. Shortly after being charged in federal court in Indianapolis in 2015, Sharp died by suicide in jail.
- USAG had received numerous complaints about coach Mark Schiefelbein years before he was charged with molesting a 10-year-old girl in Tennessee. The long history of complaints against Schiefelbein only came to light after prosecutors subpoenaed records from USAG. Schiefelbein was convicted in 2003 of seven counts of aggravated sexual battery and one count of aggravated sexual exploitation of a minor and is serving a 36-year prison sentence.
- USAG had filed away complaints on coach James Bell at least 5 years before his 2003 arrest for molesting three underage gymnasts in Rhode Island. Bell pleaded guilty in December 2015 to three counts of child molestation and is serving an 8-year prison sentence.
- As early as 1998, USAG received at least four complaints about coach William McCabe. USAG did not report these allegations to police and, according to federal authorities, McCabe began molesting an underage girl in 1999. McCabe continued to coach children for nearly 7 more years before a parent brought concerns to the FBI. McCabe pleaded guilty in 2006 to federal charges of sexual exploitation of children and making false statements and is serving a 30-year prison sentence (Kwiatkowski et al., 2016).

These four coaches abused at least 14 other underage gymnasts between the time that USAG was first notified about their abuse and when they were arrested (Beggin, 2016).

In particular, *IndyStar* details the case of McCabe, and the resulting lawsuit against USAG that sparked the *IndyStar's* investigation of the organization, as a clear example of USAG's failure to protect young gymnasts. Dan Dickey, owner of Gymnastics World in Cape Coral, Florida, where McCabe worked until fired, sent a letter to USAG warning them about McCabe. Dickey's letter is stamped as received by USAG on October 24, 1998. In the letter, Dickey describes the circumstances surrounding McCabe's firing, which occurred after he was reported as bragging to the office manager's boyfriend that: "he had one of the 15 yr old cheerleaders in her underwear and said he thought he would be able to F--- her very soon." Dickey fired McCabe immediately. He is unequivocal in his letter to USAG, saying "In my opinion this person has no right to work with children and should be locked in a cage before someone is raped." Dickey also mentions in the letter that he wished there was something he could do to stop McCabe sooner, but he spoke with Tim Rand of USAG and was told that "the law doesn't allow us to do anything without a formal complaint from a parent," which he did not have. This statement supports the aforementioned USAG policy of not reporting "hearsay," but also suggests a potential misrepresentation of the law by USAG, since Indiana law only requires a "reason to believe" that abuse has occurred. USAG sent Dickey a short response saying it was "awaiting an official letter of complaint from a parent and athlete" and would add his letter "to the file in the event we receive the letter and an investigation is commenced" (Kwiatkowski et al., 2016). In other words, this startling claim by a gym owner about possible sexual abuse of minors was filed away and ignored.

Jan Giunipero, owner of a Tallahassee gym where McCabe had worked, also sent USAG a fax after McCabe resigned amid allegations of sexual harassment involving women at the gym. According to the *IndyStar* report, the fax, dated October 20, 1998, "included six pages of allegations against McCabe with names and contact information for other gyms that had fired him or that he had left under questionable circumstances" (Kwiatkowski et al., 2016). Giunipero then saw that McCabe was still coaching in Tallahassee months later and, shocked, sent two more letters to USAG urging them to take action against McCabe. Giunipero's original fax included a three-page testimony from a cheerleading instructor describing McCabe's "creepy" behavior, sexual harassment, and stalking. This testimony is signed and notarized, and Giunipero makes specific reference to other "hearsay of sexual misconduct," indicating that she was aware of and attempting to comply with USAG's policy regarding reporting. In one of her subsequent letters, Giunipero pleads with USAG to take action to protect underage gymnasts. She writes:

> Parents from the Tallahassee area are appalled that USA Gymnastics has not revoked [McCabe's] professional membership. It makes us wonder who else is out there with similar histories that any of our children could come across. Is this the kind of organization you wish to run? If there is any other incident

similar in nature, who is to blame? The gym who unknowingly hires someone like Mr. McCabe or USA Gymnastics who knew about him and did nothing?

Giunipero's prophetic statement about others with "similar histories" is haunting in light of what we now know about Larry Nassar and other sexual predators within USAG. According to the *IndyStar* report, around the same time that Giunipero sent her letters, "McCabe began sexually abusing an underage girl, according to prosecutors in his eventual criminal case. The abuse continued for 'several years'" (Kwiatkowski et al., 2016). Despite the ardent warnings received from both Dickey and Giunipero, USAG renewed McCabe's membership in December 1999. USAG did not investigate McCabe; they placed the complaints in a file. Colarossi later acknowledged in a deposition that USAG dismissed the complaints as "hearsay." As demonstrated in the McCabe case and others, before Larry Nassar's name ever hit the public spotlight, USAG had a long, institutionalized history of ignoring reports of abuse while protecting coaches and its own reputation over the safety of its athletes.

Congressional investigation of USAG and USOPC

The U.S. Senate Committee on Commerce, Science, and Transportation Subcommittee on Manufacturing, Trade, and Consumer Protection has oversight authority over amateur sports and sports-related matters, including the USOPC and its affiliated national governing bodies (NGB). Just a day after Nassar's sentencing in federal court, under the direction of Senators Jerry Moran (R-Kansas) and Richard Blumenthal (D-Connecticut), the Subcommittee initiated an investigation to understand the systemic failures that allowed Nassar to abuse patients unchecked. The findings of the 18-month investigation are presented in a July 2019 report titled *The Courage of Survivors: A Call to Action*. During the investigation, the Subcommittee met with athletes and sexual abuse survivors in a wide range of sports, met with the USOPC and NGBs, and reviewed and analyzed thousands of pages of evidence. Subcommittee staff also completed training by the Center for SafeSport to "better understand the educational resources provided to sports communities" (U.S. Senate, 2019, p. 2). (The U.S. Center for SafeSport is a federally authorized, nonprofit organization that provides education, resources, and training to end abuse in sport.)

While the focus of the Senate report is the Nassar case, it also notes that criminal behavior is more widespread in amateur Olympic sports than just gymnastics, including allegations of sexual abuse in USA Taekwondo, USA Swimming, U.S. Figure Skating, and other sports. Institutional failure to protect athletes, including insufficient safeguards and policies among NGBs, includes deliberate actions to conceal the institutions' own negligence. The report states that "repeatedly, men and women entrusted with positions of power prioritized their own reputation or the reputation of an NGB over the health and safety of the athletes" (U.S. Senate, 2019, p. 2). In the case of Nassar, officials at USAG, USOPC, MSU, and the FBI sat on sexual misconduct allegations for over a year, allowing Nassar to abuse dozens of other patients (U.S. Senate, 2019, p. 3). As discussed in the previous section, this failure to report mirrored a pattern of not reporting credible sexual abuse allegations for years at USAG, the NGB for the sport of gymnastics.

The investigation's 21 key findings are provided here. (Note that the U.S. Olympic and Paralympic Committee changed its name in 2019 from the U.S. Olympic Committee, which is the reason for the variation in acronyms.)

1   USOC and USAG lacked adequate policies to protect athletes from sexual abuse.
2   USAG and USOC failed to uphold their statutory purposes and duties to protect amateur athletes from sexual, emotional, or physical abuse.
3   After opening an investigation into Nassar, the FBI did not stop Nassar from seeing patients or protect those in harm's way.
4   The FBI advised USAG on communications to Nassar.
5   USAG hid the truth about Nassar and prioritized its image.
6   Former USOC CEO Scott Blackmun may have made a material misrepresentation to the Subcommittee (about his actions upon learning about Nassar's abuse from Steve Penny).
7   USAG's bankruptcy has prevented USOC from taking action against the NGB.
8   USAG and USOC have been unable to locate documents removed from the former USAG training center at the Károlyi Ranch.
9   After receiving credible claims of abuse by survivors, individuals representing USOC, USAG, and MSU had opportunities to stop Nassar but failed to do so.

10 Nassar was clearly an agent of USOC.
11 USOC and NGBs' unseemly executive compensation reinforces a perception amongst athletes that leadership is not serving them.
12 The USOC Office of the Ombudsman fell short for athletes far too often and is not seen as an independent or trustworthy resource by athletes.
13 No sport is immune from sexual abuse and sexual misconduct.
14 Nassar found powerful allies in the USAG Women's Program and had strong support there.
15 Coaches liked Larry Nassar because he wouldn't ask for gymnasts to rest.
16 Larry Nassar predicted his own demise as the USAG national team doctor, but not because he thought he would get caught for sexual abuse. (He thought Steve Penny would get rid of him.)
17 Larry Nassar had an official role as team doctor of USAG.
18 In May 2019, the Center for SafeSport abruptly changed its policy on individuals published in its Centralized Disciplinary Database, while failing to consider the consequences—especially on victims—of its actions.
19 The Center for SafeSport needs additional resources to conduct modern-day investigations.
20 The Center for SafeSport's Centralized Disciplinary Database for the U.S. Olympic and Paralympic Movement has significant usability issues.
21 An arbitration panel used by the Center for SafeSport asked inappropriate questions to a victim who came forward with a report of sexual assault.

The focus of these key findings is the institutional failings in the Nassar case, such as lack of adequate policies, failure to report abuse, failure to protect athletes' physical wellbeing (e.g., lack of adequate recovery time after injury), institutional politics, and lack of resources to investigate allegations of abuse. However, the Subcommittee does also reference an institutional culture that silenced athletes, particularly over concerns of retaliation if they spoke out. During the investigation, "athletes shared information with the Subcommittee articulating the perceived threat of losing progress towards their athletic goals if they spoke out against coaches, officials, or other adult individuals associated with their sport" (U.S. Senate, 2019, p. 5). This fear of retaliation and lack of institutional trust reportedly led some athletes to avoid the dispute resolution and reporting procedures that were available to them, however inadequate.

One focus of the report is the time period between three gymnasts' reports of Nassar's abuse to USAG in the summer of 2015 until his firing from MSU in August 2016. The Subcommittee finds this time period to be the "most troubling" in their investigation, noting that:

> Nassar duped a myriad of people over his career, including patients, athletes, parents, coaches, and officials, but until he was arrested, no one had come as close to understanding the true nature of Nassar's crimes as USAG in the summer of 2015.
>
> U.S. Senate (2019, p. 2)

After Maggie Nichols spoke with her coach, Sarah Jantzi, about her discomfort with Nassar and his treatments in June 2015, Jantzi reported the conversation to a USAG official. Rather than contact law enforcement, USAG chose to conduct an internal investigation into the claim, which resulted in two additional allegations from Aly Raisman and McKayla Maroney. USAG finally reported Nassar to the FBI on July 27, 2015, 40 days after Jantzi's initial report. The FBI then appeared to sit on the case indefinitely while USAG sought to keep a tight lid on the story. Ultimately, in an effort to avoid a public scandal, Nassar was allowed to quietly retire from USAG without any indication of misconduct. Nassar announced that he was stepping down via a lengthy post on his Facebook page that outlined all of his accomplishments and contributions in gymnastics. (In true narcissist fashion, his signature block—on a Facebook post—is followed by a long list of his awards from various institutions.) "USAG's actions indicate that the organization prioritized its image above the health and safety of the athlete community," states the report (U.S. Senate, 2019, p. 7). And because neither USAG nor the FBI shared that Nassar was under investigation with his employer (or any other member of the gymnastics community), Nassar continued to work at MSU and abuse patients for another 420 days until the *IndyStar* article was published and Rachael Denhollander filed a complaint against him with MSU police in August 2016. Some heart-wrenching victim impact statements from the sentencing hearings in Ingham and Eaton Counties were from victims whose abuse began during these 420 days when, unbeknownst to any of his patients, Nassar was under investigation with the FBI for sexual abuse.

This report also includes various "voices" from those in charge of handling the complaints against Nassar, particularly in emails from former USAG president Steve Penny, who oversaw USAG's (lack of) response to the Nassar claims. Penny was in frequent contact with the FBI, and his email communications offer insight into his top priorities in handling the case. On July 30, 2015, two days after reporting Nassar to the FBI, Penny emailed the FBI Special Agent in Charge, Jay Abbott, to ask for assistance with USAG's communication to Nassar (U.S. Senate, 2019, p. 7). (By that time, Nassar knew something was afoot and had begun to send defensive emails asking for an explanation.) Penny stated to Abbott:

> We have a very squirmy Dr Nassar. Our biggest concern is how we contain him from sending shockwaves through the community. … Right now, we are looking for a graceful way to end his service in such a manner that he does not "chase the story."
>
> U.S. Senate (2019, p. 105)

In a July 29 email to Abbott, Penny also indicated that he wanted to keep things with Nassar "calm." Penny later emailed Special Agent Michael Hess at the FBI asking if the FBI could not share that it was USAG that made the report against Nassar. Penny wrote:

> If there is anyway [sic] you can not identify that USA Gymnastics has filed the complaint against Dr. Nassar when you talk to people, but just generally suggest that "a complaint has been filed," I would greatly appreciate it. It will keep things on a much more level playing field if no one can point in any one direction.
>
> U.S. Senate (2019, p. 132)

These email communications suggest just how much appearance and reputation mattered to Penny and, by extension, to USAG. If we are to read Penny's words literally, his "biggest concern" was containing Nassar's story and maintaining the status quo rather than seeking the truth and protecting victims. His request that USAG not be identified as filing the complaint indicates his concern that the organization's name would be connected to the case, and perhaps even paranoia about Nassar himself knowing that Penny had reported him, which seems logical given that Nassar had built so many connections and such a strong reputation in the gymnastics community. Penny exhibited a similar paranoia (and animosity) about dealing with the press. In a September 7, 2016, email to Special Agent Hess seeking his help in responding to press inquiries, Penny wrote in reference to the reporters that he "would like to body-slam these guys" (U.S. Senate, 2019, p. 134). He laments that the organization was getting "beat up" by the press, an interesting position given that, at that point, reporters had done the most effective job in revealing that Nassar had sexually abused his organization's member gymnasts for decades.

Coincidentally, in an email sent on October 20, 2015, Abbott thanked Penny for the "beer and conversation" they had enjoyed a few weeks prior. Abbott then mentions that he is still thinking about a position with USOC brought to him by Penny as a "tantalizing and interesting possible opportunity post-Bureau" (U.S. Senate, 2019, p. 232). In an unexpected turn to this story that I cannot quite wrap my mind around, the FBI special agent in charge of investigating Nassar and the USAG president were chatting about career opportunities for Abbott at USOC over a beer nearly a year before federal charges were finally brought against Nassar.

We also learn in the written testimony of Rhonda Faehn, the Senior Vice President of USAG at the time, that Maggie Nichols' mother, Gina Nichols, had approached her after a competition and asked her to "please not let [Márta] Karolyi know that it was Gina's daughter who reported concerns over Nassar's treatments" (U.S. Senate, 2019, p. 74). I find this line in Faehn's testimony particularly important because it reflects the danger of speaking up in the culture of elite gymnastics. Even in reporting sexual abuse, Nichols and her mother were concerned about being identified by name, presumably because they expected negative consequences from Károlyi, the national team coach. This statement also further reflects how impractical and ineffective USAG's policy was of only reporting abuse if it was brought to them by the victim or the victim's parent.

Another insight is the rhetoric of Nassar himself, through various emails, as he attempts to navigate the building case against him. I will mention one email in particular here, since it references themes that are relevant to this study. On August 13, 2014, Nassar emailed Luan Peszek, Vice President of the USAG women's program, about internal politics at USAG and his intended resignation over conflicts with Steve Penny. (Nassar ultimately did not choose to resign at that time and was kept on as the team doctor for the women's program.) Nassar expresses to Peszek that Penny does not like him, in part, because he does not "tell him anything about injuries." Nassar recounts how he pushed to keep a gymnast on the team in spite of an injured knee, since he knew that Penny would want to replace an injured gymnast with an alternate. He also indicates that the team had a "code of silence" for athletes not to talk with the press about their injuries, lamenting that McKayla Maroney had spoken to the press about her fractured toe at the 2012 Olympics. Nassar tells Peszek that (misspelled words corrected) "we keep things as [quiet] as possible so as not to distract [from] the mission of the team. The mission is about performance, not injury" (U.S. Senate, 2019, p. 212). In this email, Nassar articulates that a philosophy of practicing and competing through the pain was actually institutionalized at USAG, prioritizing performance over health and healing. According to the report, "the Subcommittee believed that it must have been widely known that Nassar rarely prescribed rest for gymnasts" (U.S. Senate, 2019, p. 20). Nassar even suggests that the team was supposed to keep silent about their injuries and that this mandate of silence was in fact a team "code." Nassar also deftly sets up an "us v. them" environment where he is painted as protecting athletes, coaches, and the program against the meddling and institutional politics of Steve Penny and others.

As rhetoric is my specific focus in this study, I will note one additional feature of the language of the report that caught my attention. In reading through the various reports on Nassar, but in particular this U.S. Senate report, I have noticed the careful phrasing used to speak about victims of abuse. The term "survivor" is privileged over "victim," and whenever a survivor is mentioned as coming forward about her abuse, she is labeled as "brave" and/or "courageous." The title of the report is "The Courage of Survivors," and the first two paragraphs include at least six references to courage or synonyms of courage. Especially after conducting this research, I do not disagree that victims were in such peril when coming forward about abuse, it required great courage. I understand and respect the courageous act of speaking up about abuse. So why does this term in this context fall a bit flat for me? Perhaps because courage was necessary due to profound institutional failings and complex social and cultural factors that ignored and/or stifled victim voices. I find no less courage in victims who, silenced by years of abusive training in a "rhetorical culture of champion-building," found they could not speak up about Nassar but continued pursuing their athletic dreams. I would hate to privilege speaking without recognizing and interrogating the systemic failures that ensured silence.

.

Michigan state-level inquiry into MSU

Larry Nassar practiced osteopathic medicine in MSU's Department of Family and Community Medicine, College of Medicine, from 1997 until his firing in September 2016. Nassar abused hundreds, if not thousands, of patients in the nearly 20 years he worked at MSU, even though some victims did speak up about the abuse. Michigan's Attorney General appointed an independent special counsel to investigate MSU's handling of the Nassar case on January 27, 2018. The special counsel found 13 instances, dating back to 1997, of individual reports about Nassar to MSU employees. Only one of these instances (Amanda Thomashow's Title IX complaint) was formally investigated by MSU (U.S. Senate, 2019, p. 10). Like USAG, MSU shared a long history of failing to report and investigate allegations of abuse.

At the request of the Michigan House of Representatives, the Committee on Law and Justice and the Appropriations Subcommittee on Higher Education also conducted an investigation of MSU's handling of the Nassar case, which focused on identifying "policy and budget solutions to prevent such a tragedy from happening again" (Kesto et al., 2018, p. 1). The committees' report, issued in a letter dated April 5, 2018, summarizes the findings of their review of thousands of pages of documents and responses to questions posed to MSU. One of the investigation's major findings centered on Nassar's ability to exploit policy loopholes at MSU to abuse patients without detection, which was "exacerbated by what appears to have been an increasing self-awareness of his distinguished reputation and the great trust placed in him by patients and the community" (Kesto et al., 2018, p. 1). The longer he got away with it, and the more famous he became, Nassar grew increasingly bolder in shirking the policies that guided his professional conduct and patient relationships. For example, Nassar did not keep medical records for many of his "treatments," and many records that he did keep did not reference that his procedures were intravaginal and involved penetration. Nassar also exploited MSU's lack of an adequate informed consent policy. According to the report, when Nassar began his treatments in the 1990s, he was more careful to present his procedures as medically appropriate, including performing demonstrations on a pelvic model and providing informational materials before treatment (Kesto et al., 2018, p. 2). Over time, however, as he grew more self-assured in his ability to abuse without consequence, Nassar slowly shifted his conduct until, by

2014, he was not giving patients any notice or explanation at all about the nature of his treatments (Kesto et al., 2018, p. 2). Nassar likewise exploited the fact that MSU's policies did not require a chaperone or other person to be present in the room during examinations or treatments of minors (Kesto et al., 2018, p. 2). Another red flag in Nassar's behavior was not asking for payment from patients or their insurers for many of his "treatments" at MSU, at Twistars, or in his own home (Kesto et al., 2018, p. 2). (Shockingly, Nassar regularly "treated" unchaperoned minors in the basement of his own home and did not charge them for his "services.") Any number of these actions should have raised concerns with Nassar's supervisors, but unfortunately, it appears that no one was really watching him.

Perhaps the single best example of MSU's failure to properly investigate claims of sexual abuse—as well as the inability of Title IX policies, as implemented by MSU, to protect athletes— is Amanda Thomashow's 2014 Title IX complaint against Nassar. The report details a number of institutional failures in the handling of Thomashow's case. The writers argue that MSU failed to properly investigate Nassar, which led to their erroneous conclusion that Nassar's actions did not represent misconduct. For example, the Title IX investigation's conclusion that Nassar's treatment was medically necessary was almost entirely based on "the flawed testimony of biased medical experts," all three of whom worked at MSU and had either been hand-picked by Nassar or by his Dean, William Strampel (Kesto et al., 2018, p. 3). All three experts were Nassar's colleagues who knew him personally, which should have been considered a conflict of interest in the investigation. These experts' reasoning, they argue, was also deeply flawed and generally relied on Nassar's fame, stating that "they mostly provided circular justifications, such as Nassar's reputation, for their conclusion that his conduct was medically appropriate (i.e., his work is medically appropriate because he is so well known and famous for his medical work)" (Kesto et al., 2018, p. 3). In spite of these shortcomings, MSU has maintained that their investigation was handled appropriately. In fact, the authors felt compelled to note that, at the time of their report, MSU still "appears to defiantly and wrongfully maintain it did not mishandle this investigation" (Kesto et al., 2018, p. 2). The committee members write that "it is incontrovertible that MSU arrived at the wrong conclusion in 2014 and failed to properly conduct its investigation, and MSU would do well to fully acknowledge that mistake" (Kesto et al., 2018, p. 3).

After suffering through both Nassar's abuse and the subsequent Title IX process, Thomashow was told that she did not understand the difference between sexual assault and medical treatment. As far as I know, to date, MSU has still admitted no wrongdoing to Thomashow for their role in furthering her trauma through their deeply flawed investigation.

MSU ultimately decided that Nassar's treatments were "medically appropriate," but gave a different version of the investigative report prepared in response to the Title IX claim to Thomashow than they did to Nassar (Casarez et al., 2018). In Nassar's version of the report, he was advised to revise his procedures to prevent "opening the practice up to liability [and] exposing patients to unnecessary trauma," such as adequately explaining procedures, giving patients the choice to leave their clothing on during procedures, and having a resident or nurse in the room during sensitive procedures (Casarez et al., 2018). The committees argue that "in addition to a lack of transparency and fairness," giving Nassar and Thomashow two different versions of the Title IX report "demonstrates an office culture more focused on protecting the institution than survivors" (Kesto et al., 2018, p. 3). Per MSU policy, Thomashow was also not allowed to appeal the investigation's report or conclusions. Nassar's dean at the time, William Strampel, was in charge of imposing the recommended corrective protocols on Nassar, but he failed to follow up and enforce them. It is relevant to note here that Strampel was later charged and convicted on one count of misconduct in office and two counts of willful neglect of duty in handling Nassar, including accusations of his own sexual misconduct in his position as dean. The criminal complaint "detailed statements from four female students who accused Strampel of using his power as a dean to sexually assault and harass them, as well as to solicit nude photos of the women" (Joseph & del Valle, 2019). In other words, a person now convicted of sexual harassment himself was in charge of supervising Nassar. Unsurprisingly, Nassar did not follow any of the new procedures, and he continued to abuse patients without oversight for another 16 months. Based on their findings, the committees conclude that "there are clear gaps in current law, regulations, and policies that help enable an environment which, unfortunately, has proven ripe for abuse" (Kesto et al., 2018, p. 4). The remainder of the report is focused on recommendations to reform policies and current laws to prevent and deter abuse and to better protect minors, including extensive reforms to MSU's Title IX policies and procedures.

Institutional culture and silence

The USOPC commissioned its own independent investigation, conducted by the law firm Ropes & Gray, LLP, into the various factors and institutional failures underlying Nassar's abuse of athletes. Part of the executive summary of the report, issued in December 2018, argues that, while Nassar is ultimately responsible for his own actions, he did not operate in a vacuum. Numerous institutions collectively failed to protect young athletes, but those athletes also trained and competed in a specific athletic culture that was conducive to abuse and silence about abuse. I quote part of this summary at length here because it so closely mirrors the characteristics of a champion-building culture discussed in depth in this study.

> There were embedded cultural norms unique to elite gymnastics that eroded normal impediments to abuse while at the same time reducing the likelihood that survivors would come forward. The culture was intense, severe and unrelenting. It demanded obedience and deference to authority. It normalized intense physical discomfort as an integral part of the path to success. Young gymnasts were largely separated from their parents during their training programs and travel to competitions.... These conditions, coupled with the driving intensity of the cultural expectations to be perfect every day, and every minute of every day, taught these young gymnasts to toe the line. They learned not to rock the boat if they were to achieve— after years of immense personal sacrifice and tremendous commitment by their families—the dreams they had been chasing, year in and year out, for almost the whole of their young lives.
> McPhee & Dowden (2018, p. 3)

Given these unique challenges of the culture of elite gymnastics, the report argues that only the highest standard of care would have been appropriate to protect vulnerable young athletes (McPhee & Dowden, 2018, p. 3). But as we now know, those policies were not only insufficient to protect athletes, but they were also aimed more at protecting the institutions while silencing victims.

And in fact, the policies and procedures that were in place most likely furthered the trauma of many victims when they did speak up. Institutional betrayal occurs when trusted and powerful institutions, like universities and NGBs, act "in ways that visit harm upon those dependent on them for safety and well-being" (Smith &

Freyd, 2014, p. 575). In the case of Larry Nassar, institutional systems of harassment and callous, ineffective investigative practices only furthered the victims' trauma. During her victim impact statement in Ingham County, Rachael Denhollander described her harrowing experience at the hands of MSU officials in seeing her sexual assault claim through until the end. She stated:

> MSU, you need to realize that you are greatly compounding the damage done to these abuse victims by the way you are responding. This, what it took to get here, what we had to go through for our voices to be heard because of the responses of the adults in authority, has greatly compounded the damage we suffer. And it matters.

Institutional betrayal also occurs when institutional systems and cultures foster abuse and protect abusers, and when institutions put reputations and profits before the wellbeing of their members. The Ropes & Gray investigation details multiple instances where USAG failed to exert authority over its membership, adopted practices that impeded the investigation of abuse allegations, and prioritized its image as a leader in protecting athletes. For example, the report addresses the case of Doug Boger, a gymnastics coach accused by multiple young gymnasts and their parents of physical, verbal, and sexual abuse in the early 1980s. The writers argue that the Boger case "underscores the slow-moving nature of the process, the many procedural obstacles, [and] the necessity for persistent and multiple complaints" to spur action and change at USAG (McPhee & Dowden, 2018, p. 196). Boger's case was abandoned in the 1980s but resurfaced with new allegations in 2008. At that point, it then took "three and a half years of concerted, dedicated effort by dozens of women" along with the power of the press just to place (and subsequently enforce) Boger on the permanently ineligible list for coaching (McPhee & Dowden, 2018, p. 198). How many women's voices are necessary for abuse to be taken seriously?

In *Unspoken*, Glenn describes the "double bind" faced by the women asked to testify in the Clarence Thomas hearings and Bill Clinton impeachment hearings: "keep silent, or speak and be shamed" (p. 59). I argue that Nassar's victims were likewise doubly bound in silence—the silence of the pressures of gymnastics training culture and their powerlessness against Larry Nassar, as well as the silence imposed by their powerlessness against the institutions charged with protecting them.

References

Beggin, R. (2016, September 15). Behind the story: How IndyStar uncovered sexual abuse within USA Gymnastics. *Investigative Reporters & Editors.* Retrieved from https://www.ire.org/archives/30460

Casarez, J., Grinberg, E., Moghe, S., & Tran, L. (2018, February 1). She filed a complaint against Larry Nassar in 2014. Nothing happened. *CNN.* Retrieved from https://www.cnn.com/2018/02/01/us/msu-amanda-thomashow-complaint-larry-nassar/index.html

Joseph, E., & del Valle, L. (2019, June 13). Former Michigan State dean guilty of misconduct in office and willful neglect of duty. *CNN.* Retrieved from https://www.cnn.com/2019/06/12/us/msu-strampel-conviction-nassar/index.html

Kesto, K., Chang, S., LaSata, K., & Hoadley, J. (2018, April 5). *Letter to the Michigan House of Representatives.* Retrieved from https://www.wlns.com/news/house-lawmakers-reveal-details-of-investigation-into-msu-involving-larry-nassar/amp/

Kwiatkowski, M., Alesia, M., & Evans, T. (2016, August 4). A blind eye to sex abuse: How USA Gymnastics failed to report cases. *IndyStar.* Retrieved from https://www.indystar.com/story/news/investigations/2016/08/04/usa-gymnastics-sex-abuse-protected-coaches/85829732/

McPhee, J., & Dowden, J. P. (2018). *Report of the independent investigation: The constellation of factors underlying Larry Nassar's abuse of athletes.* Boston, MA: Ropes & Gray.

Smith, C. P., & Freyd, J. F. (2014). Institutional betrayal. *American Psychologist*, 69(6), 575–587.

U.S. Senate (2019, July). *The courage of survivors: A call to action.* U.S. Senate Report, Washington, DC.

6   The uphill climb forward

As I was still drafting an early version of this manuscript, a headline popped up on my screen that former U.S. Olympic gymnastics coach Maggie Haney had been suspended for 8 years by USA Gymnastics (USAG) over allegations of verbal and emotional abuse of gymnasts. The *Orange County Register* reported that several athletes, including Olympic medalist Laurie Hernandez, had alleged in hearings with USAG that Haney bullied and harassed them, including pressure to train or compete while injured (Hanna, 2020). USAG stated that an independent panel "found that Ms. Haney violated the USA Gymnastics Code of Ethical Conduct, Safe Sport Policy, and other policies" and, as a result, the panel determined that "Ms. Haney is suspended from membership, and any coaching of USA Gymnastics athletes or in member clubs for a period of eight years" (Hanna, 2020). The suspension gives me cautious hope that one potential result of the Larry Nassar tragedy is not only a newfound ability among USAG athletes to speak up about their abusers, but also a newfound willingness within USAG to listen to and act on athletes' concerns.

Jennifer Doyle (2019) writes, "It is not a stretch to say that the whole of women's sports is haunted by sexual violence" (p. 44). Prompted by the urgent (and personal) need to understand the connection between silence, violence, and organization in youth and college athletics, I analyzed texts related to "rhetorical cultures of champion-building" and conducted a case study of the Larry Nassar abuse scandal at Michigan State University (MSU) and within USAG. Based on this analysis, I can make a number of observations about the nature of rhetorics of silencing within the youth and college programs studied and the impact of rhetoric and discursive practices on athletes' willingness to speak up about abuse.

DOI: 10.4324/9781003349846-6

Athletes were clearly afraid to speak up about abuse, and in part, this was due to the messages they received while they trained and competed. Discursive practices included constant yelling and verbal abuse by coaches; belittling and "beating you down;" forcing subservience and the inability to question authority; exhibiting favoritism, pitting athletes against each other, and encouraging resentment; withholding approval, ignoring, and shunning; body shaming and name calling; and motivating through anger and shame. These discursive practices, repeated and passed on to athletes who then become coaches, underpin what I have called "rhetorical cultures of champion-building." Athletes were easily groomed into trusting Nassar because, in many cases, he was a welcome contrast to their coaches, especially when separated from their parents. Pain was a normal part of gymnastics training, and so was fear and powerlessness. Coaches dismissed or ignored claims of pain or injury, framing them as signs of weakness, "faking," or laziness. Meanwhile, pushing through pain was framed as toughness, willingness to face adversity, and an athlete's "badge of honor." Athletes trained under such conditions did not feel empowered to speak up about Nassar's abuse and may have been less likely to recognize Nassar's treatments as abuse.

Athletes appeared to be particularly susceptible to the ethos of celebrity, although identifying Nassar as a medical professional also mattered. Victims felt like they should trust and/or not speak out against Nassar because he was a doctor. Nassar's fame in his field and as the "Olympic doctor" also appears to have played a key role in silencing victims, in part due to the repeated and constantly reproduced narratives surrounding his reputation. These rhetorical practices ranged from the visual rhetoric of the memorabilia in Nassar's office to the constantly repeated catchphrases to athletes of how "lucky they were" to be seen by such a "world-renowned doctor," the "sports medicine guru," and the "doctor to Olympians." Victims reiterated these phrases frequently in the victim impact statements.

Habit and sports culture played a role in victims' unwillingness to speak up about abuse. Especially at the elite level, the cultural norms of athletic training—such as pushing through the pain, unrealistic demands for perfection, and deference to authority—meant athletes were unwilling to speak up about concerns, push boundaries, or "rock the boat." Not only was experiencing physical pain during and after training or competition a constant reality for many athletes, but they were also trained not to show it or speak about it. Athletes' bodies were overly scrutinized, leading to disordered eating and feelings that their bodies were not their own. Athletes feared losing their place on the team or negative impacts on their athletic progress if they were perceived as being "difficult" or "uncoachable." Some athletes even reported being shunned or blacklisted by the gymnastics community for speaking out about abuse in such a fear-based environment, as was the case for one Olympian who publicly accused the Károlyis of physical and mental abuse (McPhee & Dowden, 2018, p. 132). Many felt that their performance was prioritized over their physical wellbeing.

The populations most at-risk to violence and silencing appeared to be elite and Olympic-level athletes, although abusive coaching was a reality even for junior competitive athletes. At Gedderts' Twistars USA Gymnastics Club, for example, coach John Geddert has been accused of verbal and physical abuse of gymnasts at all ages. Geddert's training discourses included constant belittling, yelling and screaming, withholding of attention/approval, and refusal to legitimize pain/demanding to continue training in pain. As a result, gymnasts who trained under Geddert reported that they did not feel they could ever speak up to their coach about their concerns and that they felt like Nassar was the "nice guy" comparatively.

Meanwhile, silencing was institutionalized, lending to a sense of institutional betrayal if victims did report abuse. Policies were not only insufficient to protect athletes, but they were also aimed more at protecting the institutions while silencing victims. Athletes were actively discouraged from discussing their injuries with their coaches and with the press, making them less likely to discuss other concerns. If victims did report abuse, institutional red tape, inadequate investigation measures, and the prioritization of institutional self-preservation meant that victims' claims took undue time, effort, and money to see any solutions, which were then often inadequate. These institutional failures resulted in victims experiencing further ordeal and further trauma if they did choose to speak up. Many victims spoke at Nassar's sentencing hearings about their sense of anger and betrayal at being silenced by various institutions, while some also detailed their harrowing experiences of reporting abuse.

Overall, in this particular case, Larry Nassar operated within organizations and training cultures that were ideal for a sexual predator to abuse his victims without consequence. While victims could not or would not speak up about their abuse, nobody was really watching Nassar anyway. Nassar's victims were doubly bound in silence—the silence of the pressures of gymnastics training culture and their powerlessness against Larry Nassar, as well as the silence imposed by their powerlessness against the institutions charged with protecting them. As in other cases, without the intervention of the press, Nassar would likely still be abusing victims today.

I recognize that generalizing the phenomena described in this study beyond the specific case and sports studied is potentially problematic. However, I may theorize that the processes and discourses that led to silencing behaviors in the context of athletes' experiences within USAG and at MSU may be applicable to other organizations and sports, especially if they share the same ideologies, beliefs, behaviors, training techniques, and discourse practices. The investigations described here, including the U.S. Senate report and Ropes & Gray investigation, found evidence of similar cultures and patterns of abuse, silencing, and failure to protect athletes in other sports, such as swimming, track and field, taekwondo, and figure skating. Future studies should continue to interrogate the practices, policies, and cultures in other sports at both the youth and college levels.

The path forward

I have stated previously that I consider the problem of abuse in youth and college athletics to be a *wicked* problem that cannot be solved by one person or one study. The bigger picture of what meaningful change for athletes means is daunting, really. I see lasting change only prompted by a global movement spurred by different voices from many disciplines transforming many different areas, from policy and procedural changes to everyday interactions between athletes, parents/guardians, and coaching staff. Protecting athletes will mean cultural shifts in athletic training, as well as social constructs of "the athlete." To speak out against something as venerated and deeply ingrained in the fabric of American society as sports institutions is, quite frankly, an uphill climb. Some fans may simply not want to "see behind the curtain" of the sports they love and enjoy each season. Others find it easier to dismiss and downplay athlete concerns as "whiners," "poor losers," "snowflakes," "not tough enough," etc. than to take a sharp look at the other-than-human expectations we have long demanded of our hero-athletes. And based on this study, I also wonder if former athletes trained in rhetorical cultures of champion-building are even able to question those enduring training cultures. As Olympic gymnast Aly Raisman has lamented, the culture of abuse has become "normalized" in the sport to the point where "athletes don't recognize when something bad is happening, because when it's happening to your teammates or your friends it's hard to recognize that it isn't normal" (Orbey, 2021).

Protecting victims of sexual abuse will also mean cultural and institutional shifts in taking claims/cases of rape and other sexual crimes seriously, including this very case. For example, in November 2019, the Psi Upsilon chapter at the University of Michigan hung a banner from its fraternity house that read "You can't touch us @LarryNassar" (Williams, 2019). The banner was meant to be a jab at their school sports rival, MSU, using Nassar's victims as the punchline. In 2019, a Texas Tech fan shouted "Larry Nassar! Larry Nassar!" in response to MSU students' cheers of "Go Green! Go White!" at the NCAA Final Four men's basketball tournament (Shamus, 2019). Kate Mahon, one of Nassar's victims, was in the crowd nearby. Meaningful change for victims of sexual abuse must start with taking their claims and stories seriously, respecting the trauma they have experienced, and understanding that absolutely nothing about sexual abuse is "funny."

I return for a moment to concepts of invitational rhetoric and rhetorical listening, which I find fruitful for many of the people connected to this case, including NGB officials, MSU administrators, law enforcement officials, coaches, and even the general public. Glenn (2004) writes:

> Invitational rhetoric, then, which asks only that the listener listen, and in response, that the rhetor listen—both sides taking turns at being productively silent—transforms the rhetorical discipline from one of persuasion, control, and discipline (on the part of the rhetor) to a moment of inherent worth, equality, and empowered action for (rhetor and audience alike).
>
> (p. 156)

Rhetorical silence and listening, Glenn argues, can transform the goal of rhetoric from persuasion to understanding (2004, p. 156). How do we *hear* victims? I argue that Judge Aquilina and Judge Cunningham opened a rare door to rhetorical listening in adjudicating Nassar's case when they allowed an unprecedented number of victims to speak their truth at the sentencing hearings, offering them for the first time the agency and dignity they deserved in bringing forward their stories. But a haunting question still remains. How many victims' voices were necessary for someone to finally listen?

Policy and procedural changes are also undoubtedly necessary. Clearly, MSU, USAG, and the USOPC lacked the policies, procedures, and reporting structures necessary to protect athletes, particularly in an intensely fear-based training culture. Title IX and its effectiveness should also be critically evaluated. Jennifer Doyle problematizes the role of Title IX on university campuses in her interrogation of campus security and sexual harassment and assault. She writes:

> Title IX is meant to address a toxic, abusive set of actions as they unfold within a sexist social structure. Each crisis, as it is administered, is individuated. And yet each crisis vibrates with the largest and deepest of existing structural flaws.
>
> (2015, p. 40)

Writing specifically about Amanda Thomashow's 2014 Title IX complaint against Larry Nassar at MSU in "Harassment and the Privilege of Unknowing," Doyle argues that Thomashow's case was not only badly handled but was bound to fail its victim and potentially further her trauma. Doyle argues that a "[Title IX] investigation can force an encounter with forms of unbearable knowledge, requiring a confrontation with not just the singular event of a violation but the ongoingness of the sexualized abuse of power in the everyday" (p. 50). Institutions are unable to confront the uncomfortable truth that their institution is a sexualized space and a place of sexual violence. Therefore, in adjudicating a Title IX case, the institution will ultimately "produce the truth that the institution needs" (p. 50). We must continue this interrogation of the structural flaws and cultures of abuse that may render Title IX ineffective, specifically as related to the experiences of athletes.

While Title IX policies and procedures will vary from institution to institution, the focus is on providing a means for reporting and, based on that report, investigating incidents of sexual discrimination, including sexual harassment and sexual violence. Yet this study suggests that some student-athletes may be less likely to report *any* issues for fear of speaking up, which potentially challenges the effectiveness of Title IX policy as currently implemented for this population. In particular, this study challenges recent (and controversial) changes announced by the Department of Education in

May 2020 that, among other requirements, narrow the definition of sexual harassment on campuses to "sexual assault, dating violence, domestic violence, and stalking;" require live hearings with cross-examinations of both parties in Title IX cases; and give schools the option of using either a "preponderance of evidence" or the higher "clear and convincing" evidentiary standard in adjudicating cases (Grayer & Stracqualursi, 2020). Critics argue that these changes are aimed at protecting universities and the accused while discouraging victims from reporting sexual assault and harassment (Grayer & Stracqualursi, 2020). The Department of Education released new proposed changes to Title IX regulations for public comment on June 23, 2022 (Jones, 2022). While these proposed changes would reverse many of the controversial rules made under the Trump administration, sufficient victim protections and the overall effectiveness of Title IX as a reporting mechanism remain important areas of concern.

I also argue, as do others, that standardized, consistent, and enforced national and international policies and regulations to better protect child athletes are long overdue (e.g., Brackenridge & Rhind, 2014). Training and standards for coaches—and an oversight agency with the "teeth" to enforce them—are paramount. Decades ago, in *Little Girls in Pretty Boxes,* Joan Ryan criticized the lack of government oversight of children "laboring," sometimes for as many hours as a full-time job, within a gym or skating rink (2000). She argues that while the U.S. government requires licensing for most professions and strict health and food standards, "it never asks a coach, who holds the lives of his young pupils in his hands, to pass a minimum safety and skills test" (2000, p. 23). She writes:

> The government never takes a look inside the gym or the rink to make sure these children are not being exploited or abused or worked too hard. Even college athletes—virtually all of whom are adults—are restricted by the NCAA to just twenty hours per week of formal training. But no laws, no agencies, put limits on the number of hours a child can train or the methods a coach can use.

The medical community has likewise pointed to the need for external oversight to protect the physical and psychological health of young gymnasts, including establishing standards and monitoring/enforcing specific health and safety requirements (Tofler et al., 1996).

The Protecting Young Victims from Sexual Abuse and Safe Sport Authorization Act of 2017, signed into law in February 2018, has instituted greater protections for young athletes, including requirements to immediately report sexual abuse allegations and the establishment of the United States Center for SafeSport. The Center for SafeSport is not a federal agency, but rather a "federally authorized," nonprofit organization that provides education, resources, and training and that reviews and imposes sanctions stemming from allegations of sexual misconduct. While it is a step in the right direction, as discussed in Chapter 5, the U.S. Senate investigation of USAG and USOPC criticized the Center for SafeSport on a number of grounds, including lack of resources and ineffectiveness. To be a competitive coach member of USAG, coaches must now complete a variety of online trainings, including topics on safety, fundamentals of gymnastics instruction, Safe Sport, and "tough coaching or emotional abuse." Coaches can earn certifications through USAG's online "USA Gymnastics University," but in practice, gymnastics coaches in the U.S. do not need to have a license or even basic education in working with children in order to train children.

Meanwhile, gymnastics is a sport in dire need of a new paradigm of coaching. Under the Károlyi system, the ideal gymnast was underweight, prepubescent, submissive, and voiceless. At the 1992 Olympics in Barcelona, the average gymnast on the U.S. women's team was 16 years old, 4 feet 9 inches tall, and weighed just 83 pounds (Ryan, 2000, p. 76). For decades, the sport accepted that to be the best, a gymnast *had* to be the smallest and youngest. By 2020, however, things had changed. The average age of the U.S. women's gymnastics team at the 2020 Tokyo Olympics was nearly 21 years old. And while their average height was still slightly under 5 feet, their average weight was well over 100 pounds. Our current elite gymnasts have shattered all previous records with healthy muscles and more mature bodies. And just as the physical ideal of the gymnast is changing, I encourage the sport to consider how different coaching techniques can further improve gymnastics. Perhaps rhetorical cultures of champion-building that rely on fear, aggression, shame, and silence are *effective,* but not exclusively so. Ryan tells the story of Linda Leaver, ice skating coach to Olympic gold medalist Brian Boitano. Leaver's coaching style nurtured more than pushed, increased self-esteem, used failures as a point of learning, and centered on pursuing the sport "as a tool to become a better person" (2000, p. 226). Creating a positive, nurturing environment may take more time and energy, but Leaver notes that the authoritarian, negative approach leads quickly to burnout (Ryan, 2000). And as this study indicates, negative coaching styles lead to a myriad of other—potentially life-spanning—problems. In a July 2021 interview with *The New Yorker,* Olympic gymnast Aly Raisman likewise argued that there's "definitely a better way" than the authoritarian style of coaching—training that can be rigorous and push athletes while still respecting them as humans and building them up rather than tearing them down (Orbey, 2021). Raisman said:

> When you are properly fed, when you're hydrated, when your body feels good, when you feel like you can communicate, when you are sick and feel comfortable saying "I can't do this anymore—I feel like I'm going to hurt myself," you're going to end up competing better at the Olympics. There's just no question in my mind.
>
> (Orbey, 2021)

In pushing gymnasts to be their very best, perhaps there is a more positive and sustainable way. This requires an environment where gymnasts feel safe to speak up and a shift in long-ingrained sports training cultures.

This book is about the darkest sides of sports training and culture. Its lessons have changed me and have challenged me as a parent. And yet, both of my children still participate in youth sports. Why? Because I deeply value what sports can offer for children who wish to participate, such as health and physical benefits; interpersonal and social growth; and important life lessons like fair play, self-discipline, resiliency, teamwork, compassion, commitment, and goal setting. I, too, am a sports fan. And so, I offer the lessons of this study to other sports parents/guardians as someone who still does not have all of the answers but who believes that sports can and should play an important and positive role in many children's lives. I encourage you to ask the hard questions of coaches and owners, even at the expense of being labeled "crazy." An ethical organization will not see questions as threatening or tedious. Talk (productively) to other parents about your experiences, and be suspicious of organizations that seek to prevent this parent-to-parent communication. Manage your own expectations. One of the hardest lines for parents to walk is encouraging a child to push themselves and do their best while still letting them forge their own path in sports. Listen to your children because you know them better than anyone else in their lives. Help them find their voice in a world that tends to exploit their powerlessness. Be vigilant for warning signs of distress, and give them opportunities to simply talk about concerns in their own way. You may be the only adult listening to them.

Can children speak?

As I discussed in Chapter 1, few scholars in communication or rhetoric are specifically studying athletic training. Yet our disciplines are particularly well-suited to investigate the rhetorical cultures, ideologies, and systems of power and abuse at the heart of issues of silence and violence in organizations. Further critical study and empirical research on the experiences of athletes in youth and college-level sports programs are warranted, particularly as they relate to violence and silence.

One particularly relevant area that warrants further study is the concept of children's rhetorical agency, especially considering the large percentage of victims who pointed to the vulnerability of being a child as a reason for not speaking up about Nassar's abuse. I have argued that the rhetorical aspects of athletic training with young athletes efface the *childness* of the child for the sake of athletic achievement and, often, to live up to adult expectations. Though some of Nassar's victims were college-age or older, many were under 18 years old. Ian Tofler and Theresa Foy DiGeronimo (2000) connect abuse in sport to adults' inability to differentiate their own needs from the child-athletes' needs. They write, "at [the elite] level the child is at risk of becoming an objectified and exploited instrument of the adult's goals. These goals are pursued with little regard for short- and long-term physical and emotional morbidity or even mortality" (p. 24). I argue that children are thrust into adult roles in highly competitive athletic training and that this conditioning over time contributes to an unwillingness or inability to speak up about abuse. However, the question of whether children possess rhetorical agency—whether and how they can speak and be heard, if at all—also remains a gap in our current knowledge.

Scholars in communication and rhetoric have rarely addressed the rhetorical agency of children, including both their ability to speak and to be heard. In 1987, Barrie Thorne criticized feminist scholarship for ignoring children, arguing that "both feminist and traditional knowledge remain deeply and unreflectively centered around the experiences of adults" (p. 86). Thorne argues for a re-visioning of children's lives, experiences, and agency to "enhance feminist visions of and strategies for change" (1987, p. 86). Risa Applegarth (2017) examines one instance of children exercising rhetorical agency (or lack thereof) in her rhetorical analysis of children's efforts to fund and place the Children's Peace Statue in the city of Los Alamos, New Mexico, in 1995 to mark the 50th anniversary of the bombing of Hiroshima and Nagasaki by the United States. "Even as our field has embraced theories of agency that include objects, environments, and nonhuman animals, we still have difficulty perceiving children as rhetorical agents," writes Applegarth (2017, p. 52). Applegarth argues that although the children behind efforts to place the statue used sound rhetorical tactics to become a "powerful speaking body," their efforts were undermined by adult dissent and anxiety about what story to tell about the bombing, as well as adults' resistance to recognize the agency of children speakers (2017, p. 54). Children's voices are rarely heard, in part because of complex cultural constructs of what it means to be a child, as well as an overall status of social and cultural powerlessness. In *The Queer Child*, Kathryn Stockton (2009) finds the "problem of the child as a general idea" to be a strange one, a misconception of innocence and adult memory (p. 5). Stockton is one of few scholars from English, queer studies, and feminist studies to specifically engage the question of what is (and is not) "the child." "Scholars in rhetoric could contribute in important ways to the project of disrupting [children's] subjugation by examining children's rhetorical activity as a mechanism for engaging with and intervening in unequal systems of power," says Applegarth (2017, p. 57).

Do adults listen to children when they speak? Marah Gubar (2013) has argued that "the mere act of describing young people as voiceless can itself help *render* them voiceless" (p. 452). In relation to this study, I might adjust the question to ask, do adults listen *and believe* children when they speak? One tragic theme that runs through the victim impact statements from the Larry Nassar trial is that some children did tell about the abuse to parents, coaches, other doctors, and officials, but the adults did not believe them. As with many abusers, Nassar appeared to be particularly adept at charming adults and downplaying the concerns of children. One victim known only as Victim 190 in court records testified:

> My mother did not believe me and what I was telling her. This destroyed me.... You made it so I could not [trust] my own mother or confide in her, [and] you isolated me by fear because no one would believe me about what you were doing.... You were in our

family's garage giving my mother a hug and reassuring her that you were helping me. It makes me sick. You brought her articles you had written for your medical journals about myself, my injuries, and how much you were helping me recover. Was this a little trophy? Did you get a kick out of showing me what power you had and no one could stop you? (*In Our Own Words*)

Were Victim 190 and many of her fellow survivors not believed, in part, because they were children questioning the actions of an adult? Studying issues of silence and silencing in USAG and at MSU leaves us with many questions about children's rhetorical agency/power, the parent–coach–child relationship, the social and cultural constructs of "the child," communication techniques specific to children, and adults' ability to listen to children. The challenge is not only fostering training environments that encourage children to speak up, but also ensuring that any adults responsible for coaching children are trained to understand and respect how children might communicate differently from adults, especially when expressing their concerns.

Finally, I hope to see further studies of silence and silencing in athletic training programs, so that more voices are heard from those who have lived it, and more ears are opened up to listen from those in positions of power. While I appreciate the role that the media plays in uncovering systemic abuse, I look forward to a day when victims are believed *the first time,* not when intense public scrutiny leaves no other option. We have a lot of work to do.

A little girl is worth everything

As Rachael Denhollander addressed Judge Aquilina at the Ingham County sentencing hearing, she began her statement by proposing that the preeminent question in the Nassar case is "How much is a little girl worth?" This research has made it quite clear to me that, in the case of Larry Nassar, little girls were worth less to the adults in power than many things, among them adult reputations, institutional reputations, gold medals, and a sexual predator's desires. We can do so much better.

I began this book with a story about my daughter's training in gymnastics. As I was reading through the victim impact statements for the first time, I was deeply moved and saddened by all of them, but one that remained on my mind (and to this moment, the tears well up) was the story of Chelsea Markham, whose testimony was given by her mother, Donna Markham. Donna had adopted Chelsea from South Korea, and I immediately identified with her story of her daughter's early attachment to her and the need to know she was there in social situations, as I have walked a similar story with my own daughter. What I did not know as I read the statement and smiled at these familiar details was that her mother had to offer this testimony on Chelsea's behalf because, overcome with a lifetime of trauma and suffering resulting from sexual assault, Chelsea died by suicide in 2009 at the age of 23. Donna Markham struggled to put words to her pain because, in truth, words cannot describe the loss of a daughter, especially under those circumstances. This is a mother who, when her daughter first arrived from South Korea with severe head injuries from the use of forceps at birth, sat up with her baby at night because she could not lay flat. Though Donna Markham is a stranger to me, I can tell you without a doubt that she would have done anything and more for her daughter, as I would for mine. No amount of good parenting and dedication can save children from the Larry Nassars of the world, especially when they operate within systems, institutions, and cultures that ensure they can abuse without consequence. We *must* do better.

Research calls us to many purposes, but none has called me quite like this project. How much is a little girl worth? I can say—as a researcher, a person, a mother—a little girl is worth absolutely everything. I close, for now, with the voice of Victim 242: "Never assume a child is lying. Stand up. Speak up. Time is up."

References

Applegarth, R. (2017). Children speaking: Agency and public memory in the children's peace statue project. *Rhetoric Society Quarterly*, 47(1), 49–73.

Brackenridge, C. H., & Rhind, D. (2014). *Elite child athlete welfare.* London: Brunel University Press.

Doyle, J. (2015). *Campus sex, campus security.* South Pasadena, CA: Semiotext(e).

Doyle, J. (2019). Harassment and the privilege of unknowing: The case of Larry Nassar. *Differences – A Journal of Feminist Cultural Studies,* 30(1). Retrieved from https://escholarship.org/uc/item/3389s08d

Glenn, C. (2004). *Unspoken: A rhetoric of silence.* Carbondale, IL: Southern Illinois University Press.

Grayer, A., & Stracqualursi, V. (2020, May 6). DeVos finalizes regulations that give more rights to those accused of sexual assault on college campuses. *CNN.* Retrieved from https://www.cnn.com/2020/05/06/politics/education-secretary-betsy-devos-title-ix-regulations/index.html

Gubar, M. (2013). Risky business: Talking about children in children's literature criticism. *Children's Literature Association Quarterly*, 38(4), 450–457.

Hanna, J. (2020, April 30). USA Gymnastics suspends coach Maggie Haney for 8 years. *CNN*. Retrieved from https://www.cnn.com/2020/04/30/us/usa-gymnastics-coach-maggie-haney-suspended-trnd/index.html

Heartland Independent Film Forum. *In our own words*. Retrieved from https://inourownwords.us/

Jones, D. (2022, June 23). Biden's Title IX reforms would roll back Trump-era rules, expand victim protections. *NPR*. Retrieved from https://www.npr.org/2022/06/23/1107045291/title-ix-9-biden-expand-victim-protections-discrimination

McPhee, J., & Dowden, J. P. (2018). *Report of the independent investigation: The constellation of factors underlying Larry Nassar's abuse of athletes*. Boston, MA: Ropes & Gray.

Orbey, E. (2021, July 25). Aly Raisman still wants answers. *The New Yorker*. Retrieved from https://www.newyorker.com/culture/the-new-yorker-interview/aly-raisman-still-wants-answers

Ryan, J. (2000). *Little girls in pretty boxes: The making and breaking of elite gymnasts and figure skaters*. New York: Grand Central Publishing.

Shamus, K. J. (2019, April 18). A heckler chanted "Larry Nassar" at a Michigan State game. A survivor was there. *Detroit Free Press*. Retrieved from https://www.azcentral.com/story/sports/2019/04/17/michigan-state-final-four-larry-nassar-survivor/3498526002/

Stockton, K. B. (2009). *The queer child, or growing sideways in the Twentieth Century*. Durham, NC: Duke University Press.

Thorne, B. (1987). Re-Visioning women and social change: Where are the children? *Gender and Society*, 1(1), 85–109.

Tofler, I. R., Stryer, B. K., Micheli, L. J., & Herman, L. R. (1996). Physical and emotional problems of elite female gymnasts. *The New England Journal of Medicine*, 335(4), 281–283.

Tofler, I., & DiGeronimo, T. F. (2000). *Keeping your kids out front without kicking them from behind: How to nurture high-achieving athletes, scholars, and performing artists*. San Francisco, CA: Jossey-Bass.

Williams, C. (2019, November 22). UM fraternity faces backlash over Nassar-related banner. *The Detroit News*. Retrieved from https://www.detroitnews.com/story/news/education/2019/11/19/university-of-michigan-fraternity-faces-backlash-larry-nassar-banner/4240303002/

Index

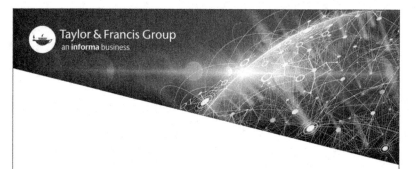

Printed in the United States
by Baker & Taylor Publisher Services